The Headteacher's Toolkit

The Headteacher's Toolkit

...

John Samuels

Copyright © 2017 John Samuels
All rights reserved.

ISBN: 1542690897
ISBN 13: 9781542690898

Preface

• • •

As a Headteacher, County Advisor and Education Consultant it has been my privilege to work with hundreds of Headteachers across the country. I have found that the most successful Headteachers develop a toolkit of skills, behaviours and processes that support them in what is a wonderful but demanding job. This book outlines some of those skills, behaviours and processes that I hope will prove useful to you.

Contents

Preface v

Chapter 1 Lighting the Path 1
Chapter 2 Managing Change 11
Chapter 3 Securing Accountability 34
Chapter 4 Becoming a leader of learning 43
Chapter 5 Building Capacity 58
Chapter 6 Increasing your personal effectiveness 80
Chapter 7 Motivation 99
Chapter 8 Managing the Organisation 104
Chapter 9 Working with Governors 110
Chapter 10 Working with other stakeholders 117

References 125

CHAPTER 1

Lighting the Path

• • •

*'The primary role of any leader is the unification
of people around key values'*

GREENFIELD AND RIBBINS 1993

PREPARATION

AFTER THE ELATION OF APPOINTMENT Headteachers often have a significant period of time before they take up their new role but are often not in a position to really make an impact in their new school. They will have their present job to do and, of course, the current Head of the school they are going to will usually still be in post. Heads often find this a little frustrating and the time seems to drag since it can rarely be used purposefully. One activity I have found helpful when coaching Heads in this situation, is to help them do some future visioning. For example, reflecting on what you as a Head would want the staff, learners and parents to say about you after being in post for six months and then spending some time reflecting on what behaviours would lead them to think this. How would you spend your days if they were to think this about you? Reflecting on some of the difficult situations that you know will be waiting for you and how you will deal with them is also productive. How, when and where will you deal with the first member of staff who treats a learner in way you are not happy with and the difficult parent who comes into school to complain about a member of staff? Time spent thinking about how you will handle critical incidents like these, which you know you will inevitably face, helps to build confidence and will help you hit the ground running. Spending time thinking about your core beliefs about learning and leadership is also useful in clarifying your approach to your new job.

Arrival

On taking up your post, everything changes and the time will do anything but drag! Many Headteachers talk of the frenetic introduction they experience with queues of staff, parents and officers from the Local Children's Services department or Academy Trust, all wanting to see them. This often results in having very little thinking time in this important initial period in post and the danger of being in an almost entirely reactive mode for the first few months after you start. This can, and should be, avoided by some pre-planning and careful time management and we shall look at some strategies for this later. Your first task is to assure yourself that the school processes in terms of safeguarding and risk assessment meet statutory requirements. You can then move on to deal with other issues.

One of the first things that you will have to deal with is the legacy of the last Headteacher. This can be problematic and deserves careful consideration. You will have things that you want to change in order to make a fast impact in your new role and it is often tempting to criticise the current provision in order to justify these changes. In doing so, however, you should remember that many of the staff and perhaps Governors will feel some ownership of the current provision and may not take too kindly to the implied criticism that immediate changes suggest. This is especially true in situations where the school is perceived to being doing well even though this may not be your judgement of the situation you have inherited. A more productive approach is often to use the language of development which may not focus so much on the change process and therefore the impact you are having, but in the long run may not result in your experiencing so many potential problems.

Visioning

Over recent years there has been a plethora of research papers on school leadership. If you Google school leadership you get over 50 million hits. Almost all models of leadership, however, agree that one of the key tasks of school leaders, especially ones new in post, is to develop and share a vision of where they want to lead the organisation. Although, as I say, there is almost universal agreement about this aspect of leadership no such consensus exists about what a vision actually is. To some a vision is just a sort of strap line; to others it is far more than this. It is self-evident that unless leaders articulate a direction or vision their followers will not be able to play an effective part in helping them to achieve the vision. Jim Collins (2001) in his book 'Good to Great' talks of a vision only being useful if 'it affects what happens in an organisation on a daily basis'. Thus strap lines such as 'reaching full potential' or 'treating each other with respect' although very worthy would not constitute such a vision. In order to be useful it would be necessary to establish what these things mean at a practical level in the classrooms of your school. For example, as a teacher in your school, what would 'mutual respect' mean for how I should deal with a child refusing to sit next to or play with another child or a child using derogatory names etc.? Only by discussing detailed issues of this nature with your staff would you be able to turn this into something practical and deliverable.

If one accepts the Jim Collins view of what a vision is, then in a school context it can be seen that the process of developing a purposeful vision must involve staff in a meaningful way and not just consist of you laying out some general aims although this can, of course, be a useful catalyst. Following this approach might lead you to take a more cautious attitude to that all important first meeting with the staff where the received wisdom is that they expect you to outline your vision for the school. Certainly you will want to begin to do this but perhaps by using a broad brush approach in order to maintain some flexibility. You then have time to talk to stakeholders in a meaningful way about their ideas and aspirations for the school. This is far more likely to result in a vision that is truly shared and therefore more effective in taking the school forward. This approach also avoids the temptation to rush ahead of the organisation which can sometimes happen. Understanding the story of the school you have taken over is important and will not happen overnight. The one area which you will need to articulate quickly and often, and then go on to model, is your commitment to the highest standards of provision for the children in your school and the highest expectations of what they can, and will, achieve.

Headteachers, of course, are concerned that staff should understand their beliefs and values as quickly as possible and are right to believe this. However, in my work with Headteachers I have found that even this can be problematic. The problem can lie in the fact that very often as leaders we don't spend enough time really analysing and questioning our beliefs and the assumptions they are sometimes built on.

Authenticity

One of the key qualities of successful Headteachers, often cited by their staff, is that they show integrity in terms of their leadership. Indeed authenticity lays the foundation for trust and respect. Your integrity as a leader is inextricably linked to your authenticity. If we consider the authenticity triangle shown below, we can begin to understand more fully how the concept of integrity applies to Headteachers and other leaders.

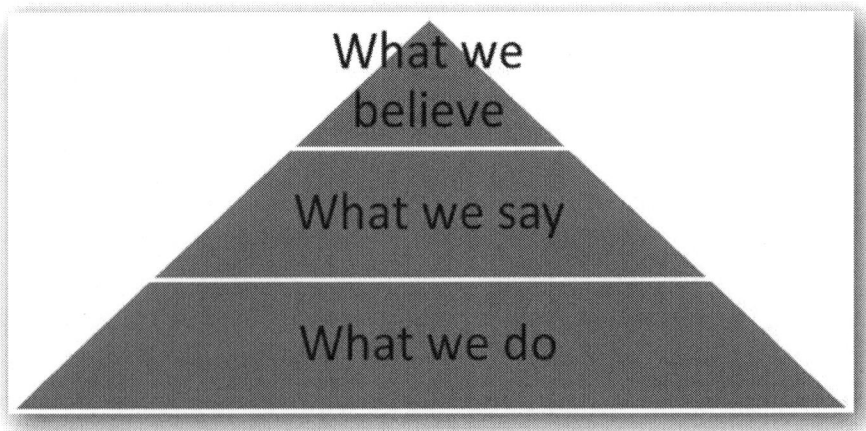

Fig.1 The Authenticity triangle

Consider the triangle to be made of three sections that can slide over each other like a child's toy. Our authenticity as individuals depends on how closely we can hold the triangle together. We know that if we get dislocation between what we say and what we do we run the risk as leaders of being accused of hypocrisy. We also know that staff watch Heads like hawks and that if dislocation occurs, as it can so easily do given how busy Headteachers are and how easy it is to miss something, it can cause immense damage in terms of how the Head is perceived by stakeholders.

Perhaps not so obvious is the dislocation that often occurs between what we believe and what we say. This was brought home to me through my involvement in the selection process for Headteachers. I observed that if you ask a number of candidates for their core educational beliefs you usually get very similar answers. My experience, however, would lead me to believe that if each of them was tracked through into their role as Headteacher, the way in which they acted and led a school would be completely different. This might have something to do with the context in which they took up Headship but I believe the other reason to be the fact that leaders do not often question and analyse their core beliefs and too often add initiatives to their beliefs which they have not thoroughly analysed, questioned and conceptualised. Examples of this would be school leaders who profess to believe in shared leadership but when questioned find it hard to actually define what they mean by it. The same can often be true about topics such as independent learning and the creative curriculum. It is not the case that these candidates are trying to deceive, merely that they have not asked themselves the sort of fundamental questions about these developments that would enable them to judge if they believe in them or should reject them. However, if a leader claims shared leadership as a belief, something that, in fact, on deeper analysis they might reject, they can get a dislocation between their beliefs and what they articulate and do. Leaders that are prone to this are often accused by their staff of jumping on bandwagons since they are seen to support initiatives that their actions show they really are not committed to.

I was introduced to an interesting technique to really establish what leaders believe in by Professor Michael Fielding. I was working on Michael's team evaluating a three year project commissioned by West Sussex Local Authority on Future Leadership. The project was led by Professor John West-Burnham. We were looking, amongst other things, into how Headteachers learn and, in order to establish a base line of beliefs, we asked the Headteachers to draw a timeline and mark on it any event that had led to a core belief in education. I have subsequently extended this by asking for key events with regard to core beliefs about learning to be written above the line and core beliefs about leadership below the line.

If you then get somebody to talk through their results a much clearer and more accurate picture of beliefs and values emerges. Often, however, what also emerges is that many of these core beliefs were formed many years ago and may be based on assumptions that are no longer true. What this illustrates, I suspect, is that too often we move new initiatives into the belief section before we really question their validity and what the implications of these developments are, as well as how they would really impact on the organisation. The lesson I think for school leaders is to ask some fundamental questions about all new initiatives before rushing to take them on board or run the risk of not implementing them effectively, through lack of real belief and subsequently being judged as a leader who jumps on the latest bandwagon! Time spent reflecting on why should I believe this, what is the evidence on which I am asked to base this belief on, how do I know this is better than what we have at the moment, will help avoid this and is a useful discipline as a leader. The timeline activity is an effective technique to use with staff on interview as a way to understand their core beliefs.

A vivid shared vision can become a powerful tool in terms of moving the school forward, offering as it does the opportunity to align effort within the organisation. Sometimes though, the extent to which the vision has been effectively communicated and shared can mistakenly be taken for granted. One test of this, and an activity I have used many times, is to ask your Senior Leadership Team (SLT) or other staff team what is going to be different in the classrooms in your school in three years time and see how much consistency you get in the answers!

In view of the issues raised above, during those initial interactions with staff, perhaps concentrating on the broad vision and then engaging with the staff in developing the rich vision that will really affect what happens in the school might be the more effective approach. It has the added advantage that staff will feel more ownership of the vision and it will be easier to hold staff to account for their part in achieving the vision if they are able to see it interpreted in terms of their everyday role.

Getting to know the school and the staff.

The other task that immediately faces you on taking up post is to get to know the school and staff as quickly as possible. You may decide to interview all the staff and spend a lot of time visiting lessons, as many Headteachers do. Both these activities are useful but prone to misinterpretation. Staff might interpret your visiting lessons as a checking-up activity which to a degree, of course, it will be. Indeed one of the new realities for you as a Headteacher is that it is almost impossible to take the 'checking-up hat' off. However, if you are sensitive to this possibility, then you can manage potential problems more effectively. During this time of transition when, inevitably, levels of trust are low, simply because you don't know the staff and they don't know you, being as explicit as possible with staff about what you are doing and why, will help establish transparency and build trust.

If you are interviewing the staff it is worth reflecting on what you want to achieve in the interviews and what questions you will need to ask to do so successfully. It is also worth considering what your reaction will be, for example, if staff complain about other staff or the previous Head. Failure to foresee such problems, and thinking about your response, can render the exercise one that ends up being more negative than positive.

Another approach, adopted by one Headteacher I worked with, who was an advocate of system leadership approaches, was to give each member of staff a half day to wander around the school and come up with a school improvement plan. These were collated and processed as part of the school improvement plan for the first year of his Headship. This type of system leadership approach, where leaders try to tap into the collective wisdom of the workforce was developed at Toyota by Sakichi Toyoda. With a skilled workforce, and teachers would definitely qualify as such, this can be an effective approach to leadership. Whatever strategies are adopted, time spent considering how they will be perceived and delivered by other stakeholders will help you implement them the more effectively.

Another observation made by many Headteachers about the first few weeks in post is the fact that staff continually approach them to seek permission to carry out quite mundane tasks. This should come as no surprise. The appointment of a new Headteacher changes the entire dynamic of a school. Even very effective, well-regarded staff feel they have to re-establish themselves in the eyes of the new Headteacher. Less well-regarded staff under the old regime, sometimes see an opportunity to perhaps influence the organisation in ways that have not been possible in the past. This is a partial consequence of the fact that a change of leader inevitably results in the lowering of levels of trust in a school as mentioned before. This persists until the stakeholders get to know the new Head and the Head gets to know them. However, there can be unforeseen consequences of this dynamic.

Some Headteachers get sucked into a culture of being involved in almost every decision taken within the school and, indeed, sometimes making almost every decision themselves. This results partly from the dynamic discussed above and partly from the understandable desire to make an impact in their new role. However, if you persist in making all the decisions, this quickly comes to be seen as your role as the leader and the staff can slip into a state of learned helplessness. In endeavouring to make an impact the Headteacher can become complicit in developing this culture. This can be avoided by again taking the opportunity to be explicit about the levels of authority staff have when they come to you asking for permission to do something. This is an area we will return to when we cover delegation. However, I think Jim Collins (2001) gives excellent advice in his book 'Good to Great', where he talks of leading with questions not answers.

OFSTED

During this initial exciting period of Headship one issue that often causes anxiety, and indeed sometimes throughout Headship, is the thought that you are now very much responsible for judgements about your school made during Ofsted inspections. Sometimes Heads find it tempting to pass on this fear of Ofsted judgements to staff in an attempt to speed up the change process. There may be times when this is essential, for example when a school is in a category, but if over-used can be very counter-productive and de-motivate staff. Trying to get staff to take a more positive approach to Ofsted judgements is sometimes more useful. The Ofsted framework is a tried and tested one in terms of evaluating key aspects of schools and some schools use the framework as a sort of lens through which to look at their everyday work. In this way the Ofsted framework becomes something very familiar to them at all levels of the organisation. This helps to develop a formative approach towards Ofsted inspections rather than just focussing on the summative elements of the process, albeit that these are very important.

Nowadays Headteachers are increasingly being given the opportunity to complete the training programme for Ofsted inspectors and I believe this is a very welcome development and an opportunity that Headteachers should grasp.

KEY POINTS FOR BUSY HEADTEACHERS!
Think carefully about how you will handle potential problems in you first term.
Don't rush to develop your vision.
Avoid developing learned helplessness

FURTHER READING:

Collins J. (2001). *Good to Great* Published Harper Business. ISBN: 9780066620992

Fullan M, Hargreaves A, (1993) *What's Worth Fighting for in Your School* Open University

CHAPTER 2

Managing Change

• • •

'You must be the change you wish to see in the world'

MAHATMA GANDHI

HAVING DEVELOPED AND ARTICULATED A vision of where you want the school to move, your next job is to manage the changes needed to get there. This is one of your key roles as a new Headteacher or indeed Headteachers generally. Experience shows, however, that it is far from easy to manage change successfully. As a leader you are going to have to live with change and learn to approach it with 'hope in your heart and your voice'! The education environment in recent years has experienced change at an ever increasing rate and the rate of change is unlikely to slow. Some of this is due to the fact that in this country education is a very political issue, but some change is due to the fact that we live in an increasingly competitive world in which our education system must be continually looking to improve in order to try and keep up with developments in other parts of the world. Given this scenario the rate of change is unlikely to slow and the ability to manage change successfully must continue to be a key aspect of your Headship.

GATEKEEPING AND PLANNING.

An important part of the Headteacher's role in managing change is first of all to judge which initiatives or changes, often originating from outside of the school, are ones that the school will want to take on. This judgement will be made against the school's capacity to cope with the change, the potential positive impact on standards and whether the change chimes with the values and beliefs of the school. In effect, the Headteacher acts as the gatekeeper in this regard, protecting the school from change overload and distractions which offer little reward. Again, asking some fundamental questions about the change is the first step e.g. why would we want to do this, what evidence is there that it is effective, how much better is this than what we already do, if at all? This approach can avoid change overload and wasted effort that staff find so debilitating and ensure that changes that are taken on have, at least, been scrutinised rigorously.

Some of the most important and long lasting changes you can make will be changes to the culture of the school. As Henry Ford is quoted as saying 'culture eats strategy for breakfast'! Changes to systems and structures, however, are fundamentally different in timescale from changes to the culture of a school. Cultures are grown and changes to them require a longer time scale and a strategy that acknowledges the added difficulties involved. Cultural changes involve changing what people think not just what they do. These longer term changes to culture are likely to be the ones that will really impact on standards in the school.

Sometimes it is easy to overlook cultural issues by becoming too quick to just tackle tasks. For example you could spend a lot of energy tackling issues such as underachievement in writing. In response you might change schemes of work, change approaches to teaching, when in fact the real issue is low expectations. Most people understand that cultural change is important but it can feel a rather amorphous area and so it is useful to have some sort of framework to work with.

A very useful tool to help you read the culture in your school is 'the cultural web' shown below which was developed by Scholes and Johnson

(2002). The tool asks you to examine the culture of your school through six lenses as shown below.

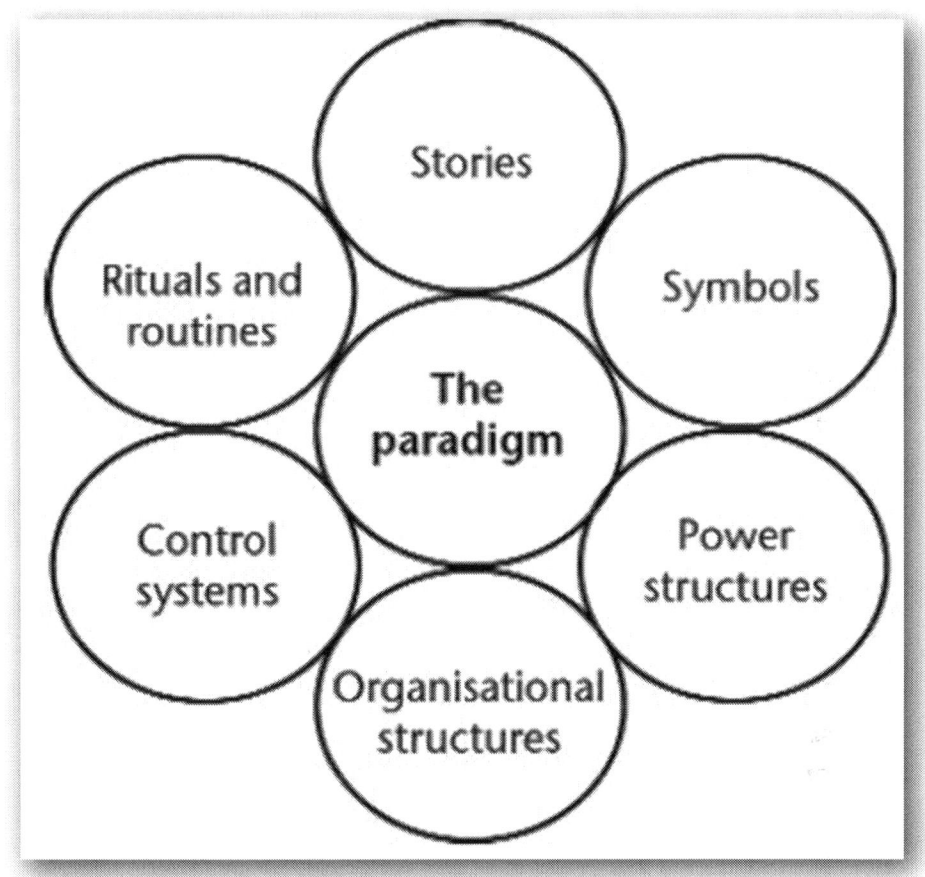

Fig 2. The Cultural web.

Stories

- What stories do people currently tell about our school?
- What reputation is communicated amongst parents and other stakeholders?
- What do these stories say about what our school believes in?

- What do employees talk about when they think of the history of the school?
- What stories do they tell new people who join the school?
- What heroes, villains and mavericks appear in these stories?

Examples

- We are known as having high parental complaints.
- Staff members talk about the Head pulling the school up from a very low point.
- The message is that we follow the path of least resistance.

Rituals and Routines

- What do parents expect when they walk in?
- What do employees expect?
- What would be immediately obvious if changed?
- What behaviour do these routines encourage?
- When a new problem is encountered, what rules do people apply when they solve it?
- What core beliefs do these rituals reflect?

Examples:

- Parents expect to find it hard to speak to a member of staff.
- Teachers expect to have their planning monitored very carefully.
- There's lots of talk about money, and especially about how to cut costs.

Symbols

- Is school-specific jargon or language used? How well known and usable by all is this?

- Are there any status symbols used?
- What image is associated with your school, looking at this from the separate viewpoints of parents and staff?

Examples:

- Smart uniform.
- High standards of performance at musical events.
- Staff dress down.

ORGANIZATIONAL STRUCTURE

- Is the structure flat or hierarchical? Formal or informal? Organic or mechanistic?
- Where are the formal lines of authority?
- Are there informal lines?

Examples:

- Flat structure – Head, Extended Leadership team, staff.
- Nobody understands the structure.
- It's every teacher for himself or herself – no sharing, little teamwork.

CONTROL SYSTEMS

- What process or procedure has the strongest controls? Weakest controls?
- Is the school generally loosely or tightly controlled?
- Do employees get rewarded for good work or penalized for poor work?
- What reports are issued to keep control of operations, finance, etc...?

Examples:

- Staff are held to account for the progress of the students they teach.
- Quality is not emphasized.

Power Structures

- Who has the real power in the organization?
- What do these people believe and champion within the organization?
- Who makes or influences decisions?
- How is this power used or abused?

Example:

- The Head believes in a child-centred approach.
- The threat of a poor reference keeps teachers working with this model.

Once you have mapped out your current culture you can use the same structure to begin to develop a picture of the culture you would like to move to. This is a powerful tool to use with your new SLT and will help you to get a real understanding of the culture you have inherited.

Specific Changes

Often new Headteachers are under great pressure to bring about improvements quickly. This can result in linking problem and solution too closely and falling into the silver bullet syndrome. The reality is that the problem you are trying to solve will often be complex and multi-faceted otherwise it would already have been solved. Sometimes the pressure for a solution leads to poor investigation of possible causes and poor planning. Very rarely is there just one strategy to address an issue and yet in many School Improvement Plans you often see an issue followed by one solution, the silver bullet. The danger is that this can lead to everybody working really hard to solve the wrong problem or what Jim Collins (2001) calls the 'doom loop' i.e. reaction to a problem without real understanding.

Fishbone analysis.

The Fishbone analysis is a useful starting point when planning to address a difficult issue.

When you have a serious problem, it's important to explore all of the things that could cause it, before you start to think about a solution. The Fishbone analysis is a tool which helps you to do this and avoid the silver bullet syndrome, one problem one solution! It is also a good tool for gathering the wisdom that exists in an organisation. It is very easy to use and in a team situation ensures involvement and buy-in to the process of finding a solution.

Steps:

1. Identify the problem or issue you want to look at and this becomes the head of the fishbone.
2. Next explore the causes or contributors to the issue and these become the main fish bones.
3. For each of these main fish bones brainstorm around each "cause" to document those things that contributed to the cause.

A worked example for improving Behaviour for Learning is shown below:

Example of the Fishbone Diagram

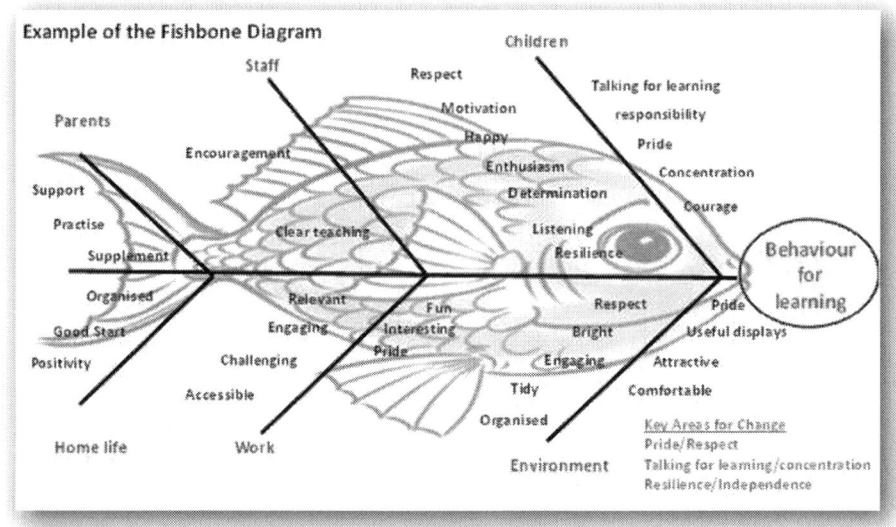

```
Staff                Children
  Respect             Talking for learning
  Motivation          responsibility
Parents   Happy       Pride
  Encouragement  Enthusiasm   Concentration
Support        Determination  Courage
  Practise     Listening
  Supplement   Clear teaching  Resilience    (Behaviour
  Organised    Relevant  Respect  Pride      for
  Good Start   Engaging  Fun  Bright  Useful displays   learning)
Positivity     Challenging  Interesting  Engaging  Attractive
               Accessible   Pride  Tidy  Comfortable
Home life      Work         Organised    Key Areas for Change
                            Environment  Pride/Respect
                                         Talking for learning/concentration
                                         Resilience/Independence
```

Fig. 3 Fishbone analysis

The visual representation ensures that all the thinking is captured. If this had just been a team discussion about the issue a lot of the thinking would have been lost as one point was made after another. Once complete the team choose what areas they are going to tackle to resolve the issue. Very rarely would this result in just one approach or silver bullet to solve a problem. Some of the things you can do will be much easier to implement than others. Where a lot of time and resource will be required, the Force field analysis shown below, will help you decide which is likely to be the most productive strategy.

The Fishbone tool can be used with different groups of staff. For example if you were looking at Behaviour for Learning, you might do the analysis with several groups, teachers, teaching assistants and children and look for links. The one illustrated above was completed by Year 6 children facilitated by their teacher.

The 5 whys

Another tool designed to avoid the silver bullet syndrome and help you dig into a problem is the '5 whys'. Asking 'why?' a number of times, a technique developed by Sakichi Toyoda while working at Toyota, is a way of drilling into a problem and really getting to the bottom of what the issues are. For example, a school might have a problem with boys' writing. This could be attributed to the fact that boys don't read and so the school might adopt a strategy of buying and using books in the curriculum, which are more boy friendly. However, if they ask why boys don't read, they could come up with a different answer; perhaps the problem is a lack of skills in terms of reading and instead adopt a strategy of an increasingly skills-based curriculum. We could go on, though, to ask why boys don't have these skills and conclude conceivably that the reason is that the teacher lacks the skills to teach them in which case perhaps increased staff training would be the answer. All of these could be the right strategy but if the problem is not examined in detail there is an increased risk of trying to solve the wrong problem.

Force Field analysis

There are many useful tools to help you to manage change but perhaps none more useful than Kurt Lewin's (1951) Force Field analysis. This tool can not only help decide whether a proposed change is worth the effort but also what the potential barriers may be. The analysis is demonstrated below. All the reasons for carrying out the change are shown on the left hand side. The relative importance of each aspect of improvement is represented by the length of the line. On the right hand side are the problems the change will cause or the barriers to change. Again the relative importance of these is represented by the length of the lines. Once the analysis is finished the length of the lines on each side is compared to indicate the overall gain to be made when the change is implemented. After cancelling out the negatives the longer the remaining gain lines the better the outcome possible when the change is made and the bigger the driver to carry forward the change.

Although there is an element of subjectivity to the process it does provide a framework for weighing up the potential gains and downsides and, if used with your leadership team or whole staff, it can become less subjective. There are several other benefits to the analysis. Once the barriers have been identified strategies can be developed to address them. This is important because, if not addressed, some of these barriers may grow and actually kill the change. Another advantage is that the analysis helps you manage expectations more effectively. By outlining both positives and negatives to staff they have more realistic expectations of the gains the change will bring and the Headteacher is not put in the position where they are seen to be 'selling' the change although, as we have said before, you have to be positive about change. This is a more realistic way of handling change since very rarely is there no downside.

A simple worked example is shown below. Suppose a school wants to introduce a more creative thematic approach to the curriculum. They may judge that this will lead to better standards of literacy, learners will be more engaged in their learning and staff will be able to be more creative in the classroom. However, perhaps not all learners will welcome the change, perhaps some who are doing very well under the present system will not. Also time and resources will need to be allocated and some staff may not be naturally good at this type of planning and may need training or coaching. If not addressed some of these barriers may grow and cause the change to fail.

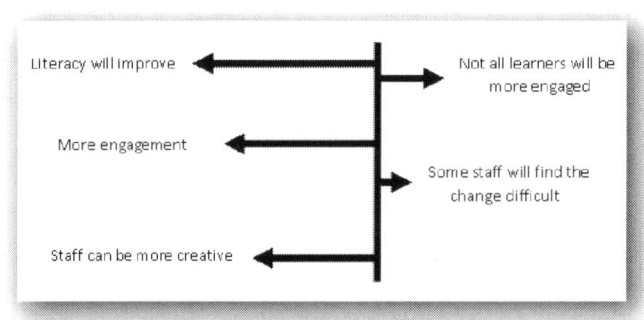

Literacy will improve	Not all learners will be more engaged
More engagement	
	Some staff will find the change difficult
Staff can be more creative	

Fig. 4 Force Field analysis

The Force Field analysis provides Headteachers with a useful cost benefit tool and although you might not apply it for every change, for those which you are looking to have the biggest impact on standards it is always wise to apply it.

One of the major reasons that change fails is that implementation times are too short and the barriers to change are underestimated. This can be caused by the new Headteacher's understandable desire to make an impression.

BECKHARD CHANGE EQUATION

In view of the amount of change we have already experienced in education it is perhaps surprising that if you ask staff in many schools how change is managed in this school, you rarely get any consistency from staff in terms of their answers. This lack of understanding of the change process must impact negatively on the ability of staff to support change even if they are motivated to do so. Adopting a model for change which is shared and understood throughout the school is a powerful method of addressing this issue. There are many models of change that one could use for this but one of the simplest and yet most effective is the Beckhard (1969) Change Equation.

Beckhard showed that in order to overcome the inertia which is always the background to change, three things must be in place. He expressed this in the form of an equation:

Need x Vision x First steps > Resistance to change.

Fig. 5 Beckhard Change Equation.

Beckhard found that if any of these three factors were not delivered effectively when managing the change process, then the change would not embed. The first step is to establish the need for the change. In my experience the best way to establish need is to evidence it with as much primary data as you can in order to avoid relying solely on opinion which so easily can turn into a difference of opinion and potential conflict. When he talks of vision, Beckhard is not talking of a strap line but a vivid picture of how this change would affect the work that staff, who will be implementing the change, do on a daily basis. Staff need to see what the change would mean to them if they are to understand and support it. Sometimes leaders fall into the trap of defining the vision in terms of outcomes rather than inputs which staff find both unfair and unhelpful. Finally, putting in place some easily achievable first steps will help move the change forward. If Headteachers embark on change without really establishing need then inevitably staff will feel ambivalent at best in terms of the implementation even if they are provided with first steps. If they are convinced of the need but have no understanding of how the change will affect them, they will be anxious about embarking on the proposed change and may lack commitment. If they are convinced of the need for change and can see how it could work for them but don't have the first steps to move forward they cannot effectively implement the change.

Helpful though I think this model is, as I said many others exist and would be worth investigating. Other examples would be the Kotter's (1996) eight step model. Information on this model can be readily found on the internet. The real power in having a model of change for your school are the gains to be made from having a transparent process, understood by all, as well a shared language of change. Thus if you used the Beckhard model, all staff would come to understand and use the same language of change, need, vision and first steps. This would also help your Middle Leaders in their role in leading change within their own teams. Although I prefer the simplicity of the Beckhard model to that of Kotter, which is similar in many ways, Kotter has some interesting things to say about why change fails. Some of the main reasons are shown in the list below:

- *Allowing too much complexity*
- *Failing to build a substantial coalition of people committed to the change*
- *Failing to understanding the need for a clear vision*
- *Failing to clearly communicate the vision*
- *Permitting roadblocks against the vision*
- *Not planning and getting short-term wins*

- *Declaring victory too soon*
- *Not anchoring changes in the school culture*

APPRECIATIVE INQUIRY

Sometimes a Headteacher might be joining a school where, for whatever reason, morale is very low. Perhaps the school has had a poor Ofsted, a succession of leaders in a short space of time or some other problem. An approach to change known as Appreciative Inquiry can sometimes be very helpful in these circumstances. This was developed by David Cooperrider and Suresh Srivasta (1987). This method of planning change has a number of advantages in that it:

- is future orientated rather than backward looking
- starts with a success rather than a problem
- treats organisations as organic, a set of relationships

Briefly the process consists of four stages: Discovery, Dream, Design and Deliver.

In the Discovery phase those involved in the change, which could be the whole staff or a particular team, gather information about the things they do best and why. This is not a superficial exercise; they must really examine in great detail why this aspect of their work has been successful. In the Dream stage, they concentrate on what they want to improve and envision the ideal future in terms of the issue they are focussing on. Again this needs to be done in detail. What would the work look like if we did succeed? How would our work in the classroom be different? How would the work we are assessing look different? etc. They then Design a path to achieve the Dream which often involves projects, actions or experiments. Finally, in the Deliver stage, programmes for implementation are designed. More information on Appreciative Enquiry approaches is readily available on the internet. It has the disadvantage that the process of planning the change can take longer but is particularly effective where there may be a sense of failure in a team or where the change is particularly sensitive. Appreciative inquiry ensures that because the whole team is involved in the process of change you get high levels of commitment.

Evaluating the progress of the changes we make.

Another reason that changes fail to embed and deliver the gains hoped for is due to the fact that often we do not track the success of the change effectively as we move through the change process. Learning, which is naturally the focus of the most important changes in school, is complex and we are often looking for improvements in key stage data as way of judging the success of a change in learning strategies. However, the time between introducing a change and seeing the impact on key stage data is rarely short and if we don't monitor how the change is progressing before we have the data, we often only find out too late that it has not been effective.

Adopting a more functional method of evaluating change can help address this problem. I have used a simple model with a number of schools, adapted from the Training and Development Agency (TDA) impact evaluation model. This is a four step model consisting of four stages:

> *INPUTS* - *often training sessions, meetings, discussions or dialogues*
> *OUTPUTS*- *what has changed immediately after the input – often changes in understanding, attitude, confidence or motivation*
> *INTERIM OUTCOMES* – *often changes in behaviour*
> *LONG TERM OUTCOMES* – *often changes in data*

Fig. 6 Impact Evaluation Model

The last three stages must be rigorously evidenced in order to track the progress of change.

For example, suppose a school wants to introduce Assessment for Learning (AfL). One important Input might be a whole staff inset day by way of introduction. If we identify what the outputs are going to be we will probably deliver a much better day. Suppose we are looking for staff to feel more confident, understand AfL and see opportunities to use it and we are hoping to see this in action when the next cycle of lesson observations start the following term. Using the model we would have to gather evidence the day after the inset to see whether we have achieved our intention in terms of staff feeling more confident etc. This could be done by talking to individual staff or using a questionnaire. Where particular staff haven't reached the level of confidence we want for example we might need to provide another input for them until this is achieved. We often miss out this step and find out much later that our input didn't work as well as we hoped. Similarly when we do the lesson observations, if some staff are not using AfL as intended we need to provide extra inputs. This method of monitoring the implementation of change makes it much more likely it will embed and have the desired effect.

Checking with staff that inputs have been effective also makes them more accountable for the implementation of the change. There are many other evaluation models which could be used but again I have chosen a simple one that I know from my own practice works. If a school has a model of evaluation, again, known to all staff, it offers the opportunity of developing a shared language and understanding around a key process in terms of the success of the school. At a time when schools are being urged to become self-improving organisations a robust approach to evaluation is likely to be even more important in the future. If the Headteacher and Leadership team are modelling effective evaluation, this will also influence the staff ethos of evaluation.

CHANGE AFFECTS PEOPLE DIFFERENTLY

Finally one of the most perceptive things I have read about why change often fails was in a presentation giving the three most important reasons for failure. These were:

1. People are different
2. People are different
3. People are different

Exaggeration for effect maybe, but so often true. When leaders introduce change they tend to lump staff together as a group in terms of how they plan to introduce it. The impact evaluation model helps to avoid this and there are other frameworks which are useful for this purpose. The one shown below was developed by Everett Rogers (1962) and reflects how people react to change.

"Early Risers" - these people like change, almost for change's sake. They are the first people you see with the new craze - often before you realise that it is a craze. Very often this group are into technology and have gadgets galore. They are a relatively rare breed!

The **"Early Adapters"** will follow the "Early Risers" once they are comfortable that the change is a good one, or at least that it is likely to be OK. Seeing the logic behind the change helps them to accept it. They often accept that there is some element of risk involved.

"The Crowd" - the majority of the population will follow a change once it is becoming the accepted norm.

The **"Legitimisers"** - found within the crowd and often amongst the slowest to be convinced naturally. They are people with two important characteristics. Firstly, they will carefully evaluate new ideas because they are independent thinkers who need to make up their minds for themselves. Secondly, they are known and respected by the crowd. Once their minds are made up it can help others to reach their decisions.

Finally, the **"Resisters"** - people who are against the change from the moment they hear about it. Their resistance may be passive - they will do nothing to help the change, and may grumble consistently, or it may be active resistance - where they will lobby against the change, trying hard to prevent it from happening.

Thinking about which group individual staff fall into when considering a change and what strategies to support them and get them to support you will help ensure success. All the tools discussed are designed to unravel the complexities of change. Change is never easy but successful leaders develop strategies that make it happen.

An alternative model that can be used to take a differential approach to change in terms of the staff in your school is one used by Professor John West Burnham (A Think Piece for NCSL New Visions course). This is the readiness and capability tool. Staff can be placed in one of the four areas in terms of their readiness and capability for a particular change. Those in area 1 are the most capable and most motivated and are potential change agents. Those in area 2 are motivated but may need some mentoring or coaching in order to be able to carry out the change. Those in area 3 have the capability but not the motivation and the job here is to find what will motivate them. This may involve spending some time finding this out but will be time well spent. Those in area 4 have neither the capability nor motivation and are problematic in that the leader has to decide if the time spent with them will ever make them competent or motivated. If the change embeds with the majority of staff, then making it school policy and dealing with these staff becomes easier if they fail to follow the policy. Both the Readiness and Capability tool and the Everett Ross analysis provide a framework to begin to consider staff as individuals with regard to change rather than treating them as a single entity.

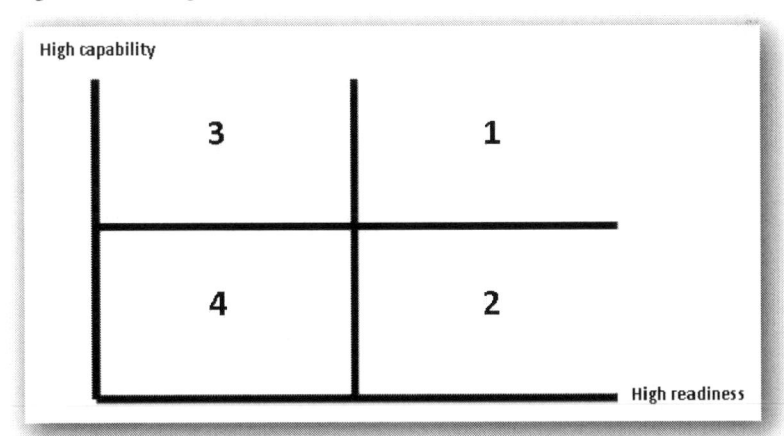

Fig. 7 Readiness and Capability analysis

Sometimes a Headteacher will be clear that a problem exists and the need for change but not so clear about what the solution and what change should be. When this happens dialogue is what is needed, rather than the discussion which usually occurs. Senge, (Senge P The fifth discipline 1990) says:

'In most organisations, discussion occurs instead of dialogue. Discussion occurs when two or more people state their positions and give the reasons for what they believe. Dialogue occurs when people state their positions, give their reasons, and invite exploration and critique of their reasons and suppositions. Positions are not presented merely for the purpose of defending them. Almost everybody agrees two heads are better than one but act as if my head is better than all of yours combined!'

Helping to clarify with staff, governors and other stakeholders, the difference between dialogue and discussion, and when each approach is appropriate, is another way of providing clarity to the change process. There will often be situations where you are not absolutely sure of the way forward as a leader and to be able to signal this to your team by asking for a dialogue is a useful tool. This is not a sign of weakness but wisdom!

Transformational or Transactional Leadership.

The tools and processes we have looked at so far are useful for managing any change within schools. There are, however, many different theories as to the leadership style most appropriate for particular changes. James MacGregor Burns (1978) first introduced the concepts of Transformational and Transactional Leadership.

Transactional Leaders work in existing cultures. They create clear structures, clarify roles, establish goals, monitor and provide positive and negative rewards. It can be argued that this is the most common approach to leadership in most schools. Sometimes Burns argues this approach is not effective. Where the problems in an organisation can only be addressed by a change in culture, a transformational approach is more effective. Covey (Covey, S. R., Principle-centred leadership. New York : Fireside 1990) states that:

> "The goal of transformational leadership is to 'transform' people and organisations in a literal sense – to change them in mind and heart; enlarge vision, insight, and understanding; clarify purposes; make behaviour congruent with beliefs, principles, or values; and bring about changes that are permanent, self-perpetuating, and momentum building"

To achieve this change in hearts and minds and transform the vision for the school requires an approach to leadership built on four components:

- Charisma or idealised influence – getting staff to identify with your beliefs
- Inspirational motivation – modelling high values and conveying an inspiring vision
- Intellectual stimulation – encouraging staff to look at issues from a new perspective
- Individualised consideration – coaching, support and encouragement for individuals

In practical terms a transformational approach could be more effective if you take over a school with a history of poor performance where tweaking is unlikely to achieve the level of change needed. Some of the work of Headteachers in Inner City Academies could be characterised as transformational. Transformational leaders operate at the higher levels of the Maslow (1943) hierarchy and thus need to establish and maintain high levels of authenticity.

Fig 8. Maslow's Hierarchy

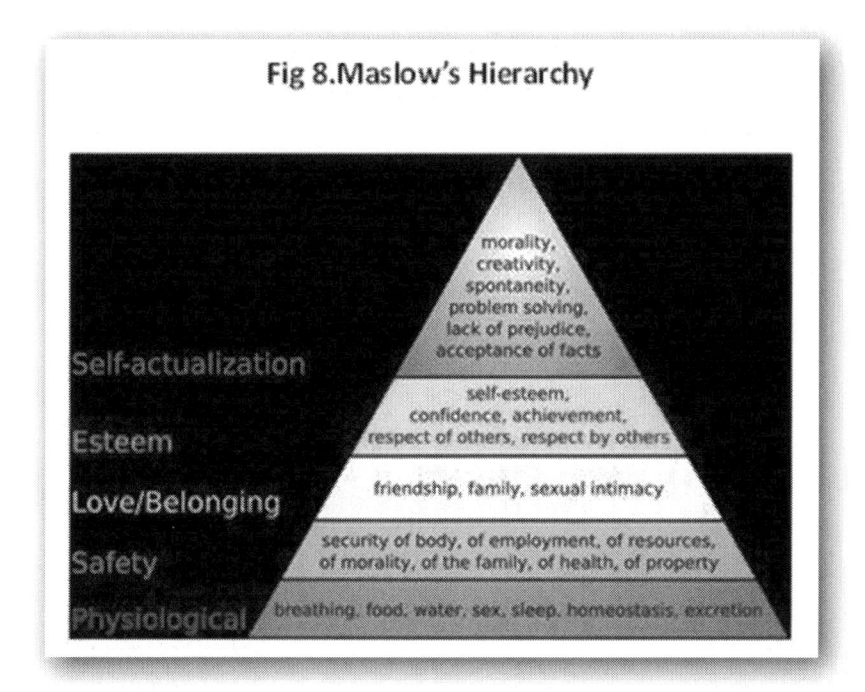

- Self-actualization: morality, creativity, spontaneity, problem solving, lack of prejudice, acceptance of facts
- Esteem: self-esteem, confidence, achievement, respect of others, respect by others
- Love/Belonging: friendship, family, sexual intimacy
- Safety: security of body, of employment, of resources, of morality, of the family, of health, of property
- Physiological: breathing, food, water, sex, sleep, homeostasis, excretion

In practical terms the language of transformational leaders is very different from transactional leaders. Often transactional leaders will use phrases such as *must do.., have to…, need to…… etc.*

Transformational leaders would be using language such as *we have the opportunity to…, only the best will be good enough for…… etc*

Transformational language comes easily to some leaders but others need to develop the ability to talk to staff in this way. Reminding staff how important what they do is, and the high responsibilities they have in terms of preparing future generations, can be much more motivating than using the threat of Ofsted to introduce change.

Long Term Planning

Many of the changes that Headteachers end up managing originate from outside the school. Developing a long term plan and strategy is very difficult because of the rate of change in education and the levels of uncertainty. However, having a long term plan can help avoid making changes and reacting to change in a way that damages the school in the long term. In developing a strategic plan all Headteachers must have a political awareness of what changes outside of the school's control, may still impact on it. The scenario planning model shown below is a useful one in terms of developing a strategic plan for the school.

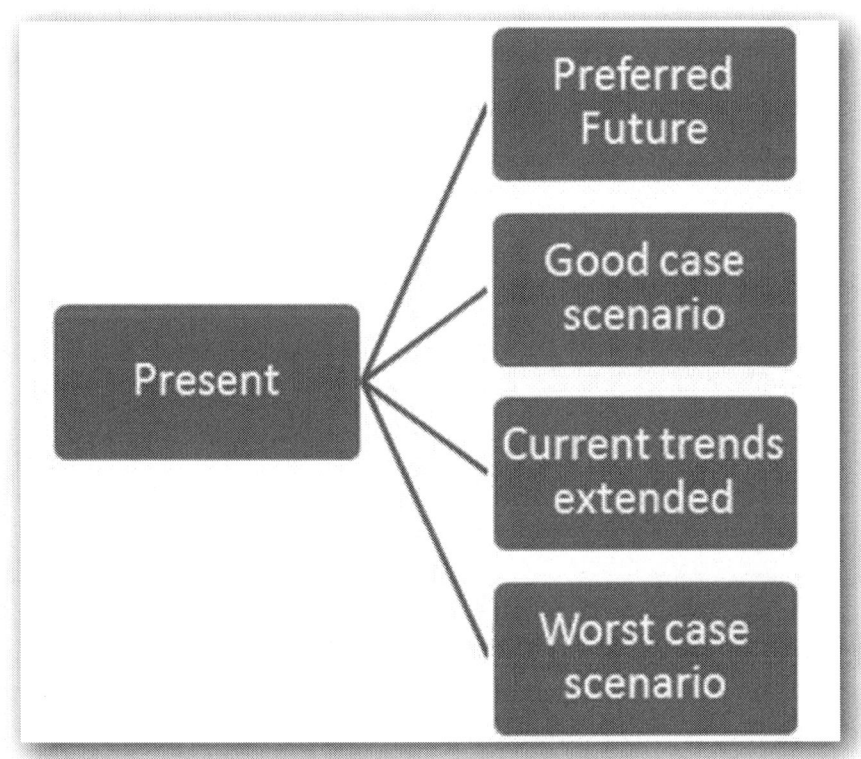

Fig. 9 Model for Scenario Planning.

- Step 1 is to describe the scenarios you have created. What would they look like for your school?
- Step 2. Look at all the actions and priorities on your current SIP. Do they take you towards your desired future or away from it?
- Step 3. Develop a strategy and plan.

The analysis below might be helpful in identifying the key issues and decisions going forward:

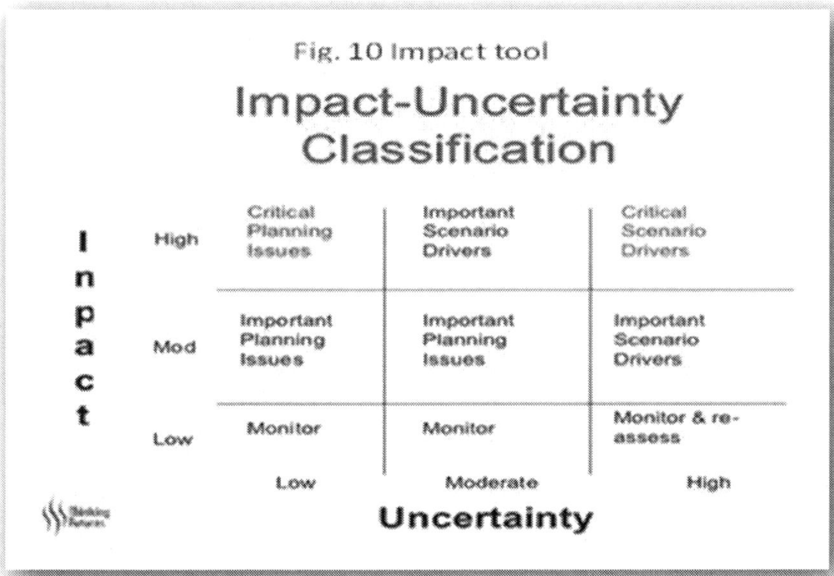

Fig. 10 Impact tool

Impact-Uncertainty Classification

Impact	Low Uncertainty	Moderate Uncertainty	High Uncertainty
High	Critical Planning Issues	Important Scenario Drivers	Critical Scenario Drivers
Mod	Important Planning Issues	Important Planning Issues	Important Scenario Drivers
Low	Monitor	Monitor	Monitor & re-assess

IMPLEMENTING THE STRATEGY.
Once a strategy has been developed the Headteacher will need to continually reinforce the plan with staff through a series of strategic conversations. These conversations should be planned and given a high priority since they serve to motivate and gain commitment to the plan.

The Harvard Business review (Strategic Leadership- The Essential skills 2013) published an interesting article on the six skills needed for strategic planning. These include:

Anticipating what might happen.

Challenging the status quo. Challenge assumptions.

Interpreting what is happening outside the school. Recognise patterns

Making decisions. In uncertain times, decision makers may have to make tough calls with incomplete information, and often they must do so quickly. But strategic thinkers insist on multiple options at the outset and don't get prematurely locked into simplistic go/no-go choices.

Building alignment. Strategic leaders must be adept at finding common ground and achieving buy-in among stakeholders who have disparate views and agendas. This requires active outreach. Success depends on proactive communication, trust building, and frequent engagement.

Learning. Strategic leaders are the focal point for organizational learning. They promote a culture of inquiry, and they search for the lessons in both successful and unsuccessful outcomes.

These are key skills needed for effective strategic planning and ones that successful Headteachers seek to develop.

Key points

Manage and plan change meticulously and carefully!
Create transparency by using processes understood by all.
Remember you don't have to have all the answers. Others can help you find them.
Create clarity and, with it, accountability.

Further reading;

Kotter J, (1996). *Leading Change* Harvard Business School Press. ISBN 0875847471

Johnson S, (1998) *Who moved my cheese?* Publisher: Vermilion. ISBN 0091816971

Covey S, (2006). *The 8th Habit: From effectiveness to greatness.* Simon & Schuster.

CHAPTER 3

Securing Accountability

• • •

'To ask well is to know much'

AFRICAN PROVERB

HAVING ARTICULATED A COMPELLING, CLEAR and shared vision for taking the school forward and developed strategies for managing the necessary changes effectively, it is reasonable for the Headteacher to expect staff to be accountable for playing their part in helping the school to realise the vision. Securing accountability is a very important part your role and is one of the six areas of the original Headteacher Standards developed by the National College of School Leadership which have subsequently been updated. When newly appointed Headteachers were surveyed by the Hay group, however, this was the area of the six that caused the most difficulty and the area they felt least prepared for. Unfortunately this is often indicative of the fact that they have had poor experiences themselves. Indeed accountability systems in education do not seem to have had a happy history, as they have often been imposed on the profession in less than supportive circumstances. The present model, however, offers opportunities to improve on previous systems and is based on the teaching standards. Schools will have more freedom to develop their own policies for Performance Management although they will be expected to produce a written appraisal for each member of staff assessing their performance as well as the development needs of the member of staff and, where appropriate, a pay recommendation.

The main problem in the past was that often not enough time was devoted to securing accountability and there was sometimes an assumption that people will just feel accountable as if this comes with the job! There is also sometimes the mistaken belief that because there are high levels of accountability for the school itself, this will translate into individual accountability. Meaningful accountability requires time and must be made a priority in terms of your leadership. Securing accountability and the momentum and alignment of effort that doing so can achieve, are incredibly important for achieving improvement and undoubtedly time spent on this is time well spent. One of the first things that you can do to make accountability systems more effective is to discuss with staff what accountability means in your school. Accountability is often seen by staff as everything from blameworthiness to answerability. Until there is some clarity about what the process is people will be unable to engage effectively with whatever system is used.

The importance of Line Management

The minimum amount of time under present arrangements would be a cycle of initial meeting to decide targets, a mid-year review and a final review meeting. In my experience the effectiveness of the arrangement varies from school to school but rarely really delivers the gains that are possible. Adopting a system of line management can deliver these gains. Line management is a process with which people in industry are very familiar and one which we are becoming more familiar with in education. The National Strategies website for example states that effective line management is critical to success at all levels within a school and line management meetings should take place monthly.

Line management would typically entail more frequent meetings between the line manager and the person they are managing than would be the case with performance management. This model of more regular meetings is being developed in a number of schools with the introduction of progress meetings where the line manager and a teacher focus on the progress of children in the teacher's class. Progress meetings are proving of great value in terms of improving accountability and raising standards. However, there are potential problems with regard to running performance management and line management side by side without aligning the two systems. One way of doing this is to ensure that the person who does the line management is also responsible for the performance management. If this does not happen there are inevitably time-consuming issues related to communication between the two managers and an increased risk of misunderstandings and a lack of clarity about who the person being managed is accountable to and for what. Aligning the systems might seem the obvious solution but many schools have not done so. This can be as a result of being tied into leadership structures that were not designed to achieve this and may require the Head to consider new structures.

Another issue to think about is how many people one person can line/performance manage effectively given the time available to them. Often accountability structures are the result of just dividing up the responsibilities between the Senior Leadership Team on an ad hoc basis without any thought given to the effectiveness of the arrangement. When this is the case people are often just going through the motions, because they do not have time to do anything else, in order to meet statutory requirements rather than developing a productive relationship. One area where this often occurs is the line management of teaching assistants where one person, sometimes the SENCO, may find themselves responsible for all the line management. Teaching assistants can be a very valuable resource but we know from the Sutton Trust (2014) research on the effectiveness of pupil premium interventions, that they need to be deployed effectively and this requires effective line management and a structure that can deliver this. Another potential pitfall is in terms of structures where staff responsibilities overlap. When this occurs it is essential to establish the extent of the authority of staff if they are to be held to account effectively. For example, if a school has a KS2 co-ordinator and a Literacy co-ordinator it would be necessary to establish which is responsible for standards in literacy and which has the greater authority should there be disagreement about strategy. Without this clarity neither can be held to account effectively for improving standards in this area. Many of the co-ordinator roles in schools raise the same issue.

GETTING THE PROCESSES RIGHT AND DEVELOPING THE SKILLS FOR LINE MANAGEMENT

Having put an appropriate structure for achieving accountability in place the task is now to ensure that the process is carried out effectively. Too often in the past performance management interviews turned into opportunities for those being managed to transfer all their problems, and thus their accountabilities to their manager. The manager can easily slip into becoming complicit in this process by offering a series of solutions to the problems. This sort of interaction disempowers the person being managed and develops an ethos of learned helplessness. Although giving advice and answers might be appropriate for inexperienced staff, for the majority the process has to be one that supports them in coming up with their own answers. The skills needed to achieve this are related to active listening and asking good questions. The purpose of the listening and questioning is to help the member of staff think of new strategies where others may have failed and to ensure a rigorous approach to evidencing what happens as a result of any new approaches. After such a process the problems are left with the member of staff, so they are accountable but they leave the meeting knowing the strategies they will employ to address the issues they face and knowing their manager is happy with these strategies. This is far more motivating than leaving a rather unfocussed discussion, which staff frequently fail to see the point of. Unfortunately this can often be their experience of being held to account!

The skills of good questioning and active listening, however, are high order skills and staff involved in line/performance management will need training in developing them and the opportunity to practise them.

They also happen to be some of the most important general skills for a leader.

You will also need to model effective accountability with your Senior Leadership Team. This needs to be done formally with regular one to one meetings rather than informally or with the SLT as a group. These informal arrangements often become too comfortable and lack rigour. Some Headteachers slip into the trap of believing that they know their team so well they don't really need to line manage them but this is always viewed very negatively by other staff and is not an effective way to work with the SLT.

The importance of teams

Teams play an essential part in school improvement but are often not held accountable in any formal way for what they do. In order to do this, of course, it would be necessary to define the purpose of the team which in itself is good management practice. I have used the following ten point health check as a way of reviewing the effectiveness of teams and it is not difficult to develop a similar framework of your own to do so.

Team 10 point health check.

1. What is the team's purpose and is this understood by all who attend team meetings?
2. Does what the time spent in meetings match the purpose of the meetings?
3. What is the balance between the time spent solving problems and time spent avoiding problems?
4. What are the responsibilities and accountabilities that go along with membership of the team?
5. What will be different as a result of the team's work in 1 year and 3 years from now?
6. How often do the team train together?
7. How does the team get feedback about its performance?

8. How do individual members get feedback about their role in the team?
9. How has the team improved the processes and tools it operates with in the last year?
10. How often do other specialists join the team in order to help it operate more effectively?

By holding teams formally accountable for their work it helps to emphasise their importance and developing a framework like the one above is a practical way to do this. Such a framework can also be used to hold subject leaders accountable for their leadership role.

Dealing with blocking.

The main focus of the accountability conversations you have as a Headteacher should always be the learner's progress, using appropriate progress data as the main source of evidence. The data available needs to be reliable or this will distort the whole accountability process. Given the reduction in the number of statutory tests in recent years and the reduced access to School Improvement Partners, it is crucial that schools develop some method of benchmarking their judgments with regard to children's progress in order to develop reliable data sets. Networking with other schools could provide a framework for this essential activity.

Sometimes when trying to hold a member of staff to account you may meet some blocking. This will often but not exclusively take the form of failure to take responsibility; 'The problem is the children in this class… the lack of time or resources I have….' Fortunately this does not occur very often but it important to understand how to deal with blocking. Typical blocking techniques include:

* Failure to take responsibility
* Changing the subject
* Compliance
* Flooding with detail

There are well known techniques for dealing with blocking. The way to deal with blocking assertively is to name the blocking technique the person is using and then use silence to make them respond. In responding they take ownership of the issue and you can move forward. An example might be a teacher who, when asked about the lack of progress of some of the learners in his/her class, continually talks about behaviour issues or other problems rather than what they might do to address the progress issue. If this persists beyond what might be reasonable under the circumstances, and in order to give them ownership of the issue you could say:

'You are not saying, are you, that there is nothing you could do differently to address the problem you have regarding the progress of these learners?'

You would then have to remain silent until they respond. If you drive into the silence you take the responsibility away from them and they don't take ownership of the issue. If you don't and remain silent, typically after a rather awkward period they may say something like 'well I suppose I could do this...' they then take ownership of the issue and we can move forward. As Susan Scott says in her book 'Fierce Conversations' (Susan Scott, Fierce Conversations Published by Judy Piatkuss 2002) 'let silence do the heavy lifting'. The same approach could be used for the other methods of blocking such as continually changing the subject, compliance and flooding with detail. In these cases you might say:

'You keep changing the subject. I can't tell what you think is at the core of the problem you have with the progress of learners in your class'

'You seem to agree with almost any strategy suggested. I can't tell what you think is the key to the problem you have with progress of learners in your class'.

'You keep flooding me with detail. I can't tell what you think is at the core of the problem you have with progress of the learners in your class'.

We will return to this technique of giving the person with the problem ownership of the issue when we look at personal effectiveness and how to have difficult conversations.

Job Descriptions

The last aspect of accountability I want to consider is the role of job descriptions in an effective accountability system. Often in education job descriptions consist solely of long list of tasks related to an area of responsibility. Sometimes such job descriptions can actually make it harder to hold somebody to account effectively since it is perfectly possible to carry out all the tasks and still do a bad job. If we use job descriptions to outline the outcomes staff are responsible for, leaving them to decide the strategies, the process of using the job description as part of the accountability process is much easier. If, for example, I make my Literacy Co-ordinator responsible for improving progress in literacy rather than for carrying out a number of tasks I can challenge his/her performance if this is not happening and not be told that they have done all the tasks asked of them. This type of approach also gives Middle Leaders a bit more freedom to be creative as well as being more accountable. It also makes clearer their level of authority in their role. In conclusion, it is also worth reflecting on your accountability to the staff in terms of the leadership you provide. I think accountability for leaders is about their responsibility to explain decisions and actions and to have the choices they make scrutinised. Getting feedback as leader is an important part of discharging this responsibility and we shall return to how this can be achieved later in the book.

Dealing with underperformance.

It has often been said that no teacher comes to work to do a bad job. Unfortunately although this may be true there are indeed a small number of teachers who do a bad job and it is the Headteacher's job to tackle this on behalf of the children. When these situations arise they are always stressful for both the teacher and the Headteacher. Fortunately there are competency procedures in place for these situations and these should be used. The procedures provide the teacher with an entitlement to support and an opportunity to try and put the problem right but also ensure that if this is not achieved the children do not have to live with poor teaching. Advice from other Headteachers who are more familiar with the process and HR support should always be sought.

Key points
Accountability is not about giving people answers
Agree what accountability looks like in your school and model it.
Concentrate on outcomes.

Read on:
Scott S, (2002). *Fierce Conversations.* Publisher Judy Piatkuss. ISBN 0670031240

Brundrett M, Rhodes C, (2010) *Leadership for Quality and Accountability in Education.* Routledge

CHAPTER 4

Becoming a leader of learning

• • •

'You have to look at leadership through the eyes of the followers and you have to live the message. What I have learned is that people become motivated when you guide them to the source of their own power and when you make heroes out of employees who personify what you want to see in the organization. '

ANITA RODDICK

SINCE LEARNING IS THE CORE purpose of the school a large part of the judgement about how successful your Headship is will be measured by the effect you have on improving learning within the school. In recent years there has been a sharp focus on the this area of leadership and some of the best insights have come from Professor Geoff Southworth at the National College of Teaching and Leadership in his work on what has come to be known as Learning Centred Leadership (2005).

He believes that learning-centred leaders can have the biggest impact on what happens in the classroom through modelling, dialogue and monitoring (through good accountability structures). We have touched on the importance of these before but one further insight he provides into modelling is that learning-centred leaders manage their modelling in order to support any changes they are trying to put in place. He calls this 'managing the indirect effects of leadership.' Thus, if one of our key priorities as a school is improving writing then you can make this a focus for the year; examples might be when carrying out formal observations, having formal and informal dialogue with staff and learners and during formal meetings. This will be a powerful tool to support the change because we know that modelling by the Headteacher can be very influential. Professor John West Burnham has also written on learning-centred leadership (*think piece* for NCSL Leading Learning and Teaching – Learning-Centred Leadership) and has added coaching to the things the Headteacher can do to impact on learning in the classroom. I believe this is an important addition to how we think of Learning Centred Leadership and it is certainly important for Heads to be able to coach staff, especially the members of their SLT.

A DIALOGUE ABOUT LEARNING.

Learning is a complex process and one we are still working to understand. Because of this there is often no agreed language of learning which teachers, students and parents can share unless the Headteacher helps create one. In doing so there is huge potential for raising standards. This shared language may consist of just thirty or forty key words that are shared between teachers, learners and parents such as the two shown below based on Bloom's taxonomy.

The Headteacher's Toolkit

Fig. 11 Learning model and shared language based on Blooms developed at St John Evangelist Catholic Primary School, Islington.

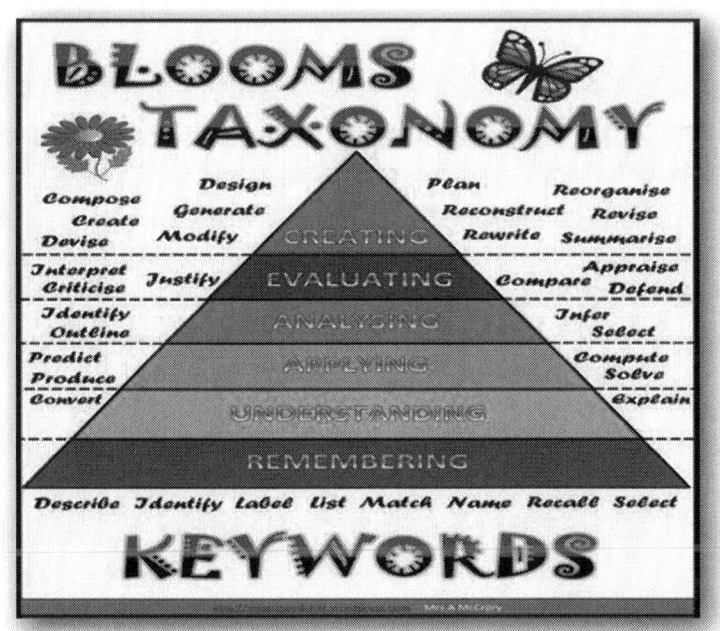

Fig. 12 Learning model and shared language based on Bloom's

Teachers try to use these words in Learning Objectives and feedback and check with children that they have a clear understanding of the learning word and process. By choosing words that regularly occur in examinations this helps avoid the problem of children not understanding clearly what they are being asked to do in an examination. It is also a very effective way of developing more independent learners when learners actually have a clearer understanding of learning. Similarly, parents are able to support their children's learning more effectively if they have a greater understanding of the learning process. The model should be displayed in all classrooms and, in time, will become well understood by both staff and children.

Although there are no definitive models of learning, looking at the research can help Headteachers begin this process of building a shared understanding and language around learning.

Bloom's taxonomy was developed by Benjamin Bloom (1956). In 2001 a revised taxonomy, expressed as verbs was developed by Anderson and Krathwohl (2001). Biggs and Collis (1982) built on the work of Bloom and developed Solo taxonomy which is widely used in New Zealand. I have worked with schools which start to work with models such as Bloom's taxonomy or Solo taxonomy and go on to develop their own model, based on a structure and vocabulary they are happy with and feel is appropriate for their students. This is then displayed in every classroom and forms the basis of the dialogue about learning. The vocabulary is used in learning objectives and feedback and, over a period of time, students gain a much better cognitive understanding of their learning and staff feel far more confident that they are doing a good job. There are some wonderful resources available on the internet, such as lists of Bloom's questions and verbs, to support this process. The average teacher asks over 400 questions a day, very few of which require higher level thinking. In my experience the use of Bloom's will transform this and improve learning. The illustrations below give a visual impression of the Bloom's and Solo taxonomies.

Changes to Bloom's

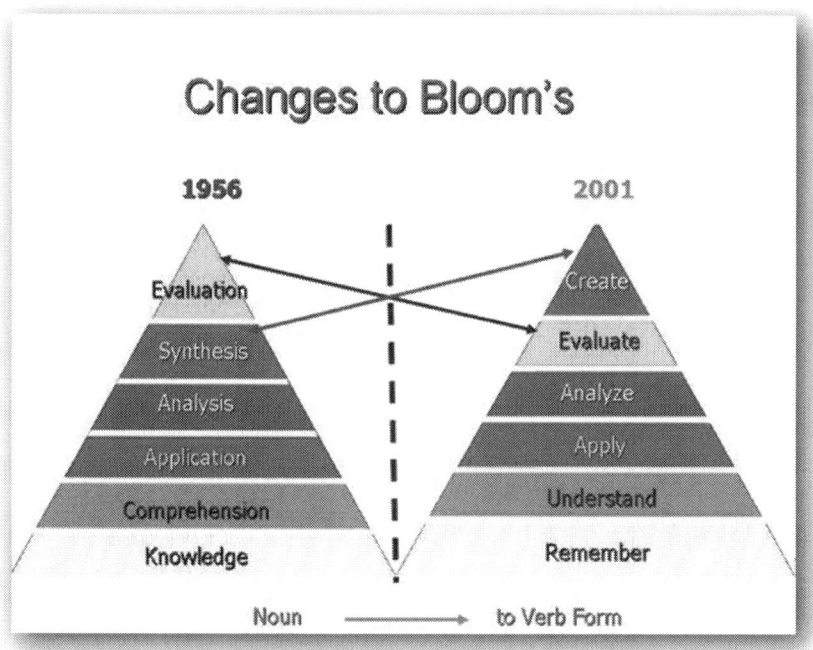

1956 → **2001**

Evaluation → Create
Synthesis → Evaluate
Analysis → Analyze
Application → Apply
Comprehension → Understand
Knowledge → Remember

Noun ⟶ to Verb Form

Fig.13 Changes to Blooms taxonomy

SOLO TAXONOMY
(after Biggs and Collis 1982)

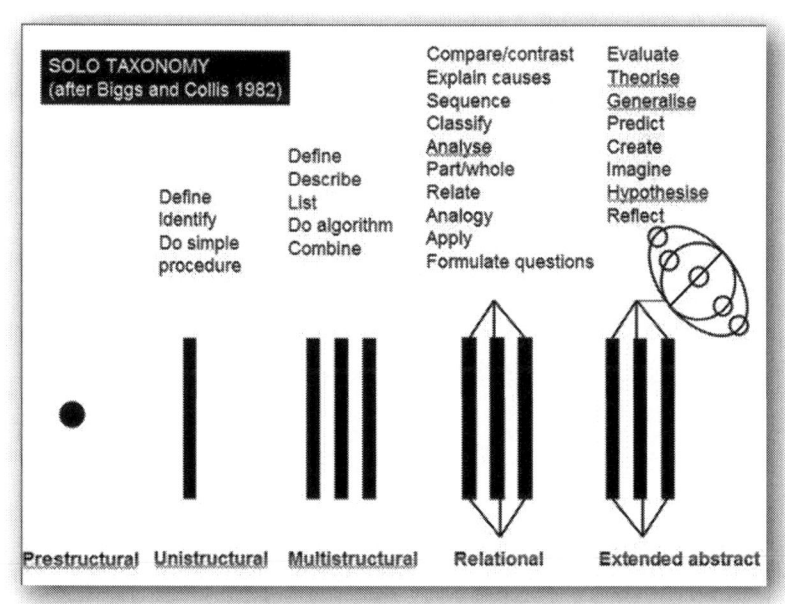

Prestructural	Unistructural	Multistructural	Relational	Extended abstract
	Define Identify Do simple procedure	Define Describe List Do algorithm Combine	Compare/contrast Explain causes Sequence Classify Analyse Part/whole Relate Analogy Apply Formulate questions	Evaluate Theorise Generalise Predict Create Imagine Hypothesise Reflect

Fig.14 Solo Taxonomy

Developing a shared language and understanding of learning offers a number of really important advantages some of which are listed below:

- Children would have a greater understanding of what learning involved and be empowered to be independent learners.
- Opportunities for developing meta-cognition would be increased.
- Teachers would be more confident that they were extending children's learning.
- Professional learning would be more focussed and effective.
- Learning objectives would be more fully understood by both teachers and learners.
- Feedback would be more fully understood by children and therefore more useful.
- Parents could support learning more effectively.

Both Bloom's and Solo taxonomies promote higher level thinking. They also demonstrate that all children can think at higher levels if the context of the learning is appropriate. For example five year old children being read a story can be asked how they think it will end and why they think this (synthesis) or which character they like best and why. This is important in raising expectations and showing all children can achieve.

After developing his taxonomy Bloom (1968) and his co-workers went on to explore the most effective conditions for learning. His results are summarised in the graph below.

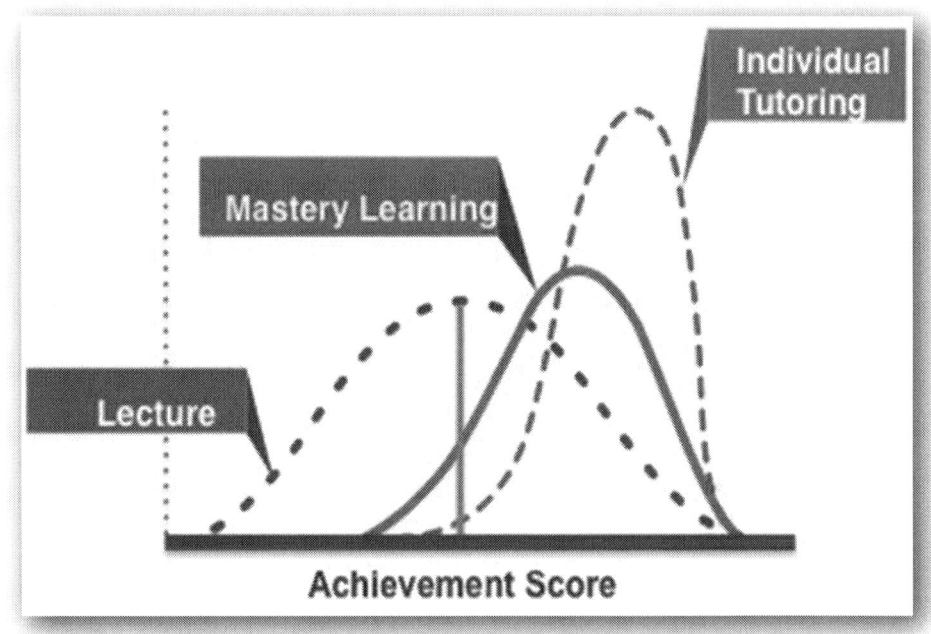

Fig. 15 Bloom's research into effective learning.

Unsurprisingly he found that the most effective arrangement was one-to-one learning. He then asked himself which elements of 1:1 learning could be brought into the normal classroom. He described this as mastery learning which is now the basis of new learning approaches associated with the new national curriculum. He noticed that in one-to-one situations teachers rarely moved on to new learning until the learner had mastered the concept being covered. This was especially important in mathematics and science where learning is sequential and builds on previous understanding.

This was translated into an approach in the normal classroom where the teacher does not move on until at least 85% of the learners have mastered the learning and that future learning will revisit the topic for those that have not mastered it. This interleaving was re-teaching, not a repeat of what happened before. The other observation that Bloom made was that in a 1:1 situation very few learners, many of them classed as low ability, failed to reach the average level of learners in a traditional classroom. This is reflected in the much higher expectations of what learners can achieve, which we see in the new national curriculum. Higher level thinking and problem solving are key to Bloom's concept of mastery learning.

Carol Dweck's (2006) work on Mindset also builds on Bloom's higher level thinking in that it is essential that learners struggle to learn on occasion if they are to develop growth mindsets. Higher level thinking activities make this much more likely to happen rather than focussing on the knowledge, understand and apply levels where the learner is not involved in such challenging activities.

Building your knowledge base.

One of the questions I sometimes ask when working with Senior Leadership Teams is how does the team build their own knowledge base about teaching and learning within the school. Often the response will be about lesson observation and the dialogue that follows. However, if you ask staff in the same school their view about lesson observations, they often have a very different perspective and view them as an example of the SLT working in Ofsted mode. I think it is very difficult to build improved teaching and learning with lesson observation as your main strategy because people tend to be risk averse when being monitored and not really in development mode. Thus, often what you observe and end up discussing is something a teacher knows very well because it will be something they view as tried and tested. Improving teaching and learning, however, is about doing things differently in the classroom and taking risks in the search for improvement. In view of this the problem with relying on lesson observation, only carried out by the SLT, to build capacity, becomes obvious. Some schools I have worked with have used peer observation as a method of building the knowledge-base about teaching and learning. They have used a protocol which completely separates this activity from any form of monitoring and have not involved the SLT in the observations in order to try and reinforce this protocol. The teachers concerned in the peer observation were all trained in coaching techniques in order to understand that the best way to support somebody's learning in these situations is sometimes to ask a good question rather than provide praise or sympathy, useful though these may be sometimes!

The use of video, where the person being videoed has complete ownership of the video recording but may choose to discuss it with a coach, is another strategy I have seen work. This method is being increasingly used to improve teaching and learning and has great potential. In a sense it is the 'purest' type of lesson observation since nobody else is in the room and affecting the usual dynamic between teacher and class. This assumes that the camera used is unobtrusive but the technology to achieve this is readily available and relatively cheap. Indeed, recently, many staff have taken to using an iPad to record lessons

COLLABORATIVE LESSON PLANNING.

Joyce and Showers (1996) in their book 'The evolution of coaching' argue that the most successful context in which to coach is when staff are co-planning work. Their belief is that in this situation staff are more comfortable providing the sort of challenge that is most useful for learning through coaching. ' Research lessons,' an NCTL initiative, and 'Lesson Study' a similar initiative developed within the National Strategies, provide a framework for this type of joint planning (The internet has a lot of information on Research Lessons and Lesson Study, including examples of their use). In both models staff work together to plan an input that will be delivered in a way that is different from the approach the teacher would usually have taken or has taken in the past. An example might be a topic that they have never been entirely happy teaching.

The teacher is supported in this planning by one or two colleagues depending on which of the models is used. The reason for involving other colleagues is to reduce the risk averseness so that the teacher sees this as a joint learning activity not a pass/ fail activity which puts them at risk.

When planning, they focus on a small number of learners e.g. three, and the detailed planning for the new approach is focussed around these three learners. (Planning templates are available in 'Lesson Study': a handbook published by Lesson Study UK) The reason for this is that the observations, carried out by the teacher and at least one colleague, can be focussed on these children. The learners can also be interviewed afterwards about their experience in the lesson. This approach ensures a rich, focussed discussion about the learning that took place rather than a more generalised discussion that can occur when talking about class reaction rather than that of individual learners. Sometimes it might be useful to choose the learners for a specific reason from the teaching group. If, for example, the reason the teacher would like to change the way the lesson is delivered is because they feel in the past it has not stretched the higher ability learners, then they might choose to use three high ability learners to focus on. Equally it could be three special needs learners if they were concerned about their learning using their current approach. If there is no particular focus then the three learners could be chosen to represent the full ability range. At the end, when the new approach has been tried and all the evidence gathered is discussed, the teacher decides on any permanent changes to the way this work is taught in the future and any general implications for their teaching. This sort of action-research approach is very effective in developing reflective practitioners but would, of course, require the backing of the Headteacher in terms of resource allocation if it is to happen. However, there is an increasing body of research supporting this method for improving teaching and learning.

In the Far East there is more of a tendency for teachers to focus in on very small detailed elements of curriculum delivery in their professional development discussions. Thus, for example, a group of teachers might discuss the best way to introduce fractions to children in the first ten minutes of the topic or how to introduce fronted adverbials at the beginning of a lesson. This deeper focus on learning over a short period can result in a richer discussion.

Maintaining your credibility.

Most Headteachers will have been very effective in the classroom at some stage in their career in order to get where they have. In order to lead learning, however, you must maintain this credibility. This does not necessarily mean that they have to teach but it does mean that on those occasions when they are in teaching mode, for example when leading assemblies or inset days, they realise the importance of doing a good job. It is no good telling staff to be enthusiastic and engaging and failing to be so yourself! They can also maintain credibility by supporting involvement in initiatives and networks which enhance what the school wants to do in terms of developing learning. This can help make the school a dynamic and exciting place to work for staff, both present and potential.

Developing the language of learning.

The language we use as leaders has often evolved from habits developed over a number of years. Sometimes that language can be counter-cultural. An example would be that almost all Headteachers would say that high expectations are important but they may talk about children being of low ability rather than low attaining. There is something global about being low ability which is not as pronounced when we talk about low attainment in a particular area. Similarly we might want our staff to take more risks in the classroom but our language could be counter-cultural. As has been said previously, given that staff watch and listen to Headteachers like hawks it is as well to consider the effects of the language we use. Some examples are shown below:

Existing Cultures	Learning Cultures
Ability	Attainment
Work Scrutiny	Learning Search
Lesson Observation	Learning audit
Homework	Home learning

- Teaching assistant | Learning support assistant
- Performance Management | Improvement of personal effectiveness
- Feedback | Feedforward (see Marshall Ward feedforward tool)
- Professional Development | Professional Learning
- Outstanding | Excellent
- Monitor | Review

Pupil Voice

Another key aspect of learning-centred leadership is how you engage with the learners. Some aspects of this engagement have come to be known as pupil voice. Pupil voice has, I believe, a huge potential to improve learning if used effectively.

Pupil voice, in the form of school councils, have existed for some time and have often been involved in very worthy but perhaps not key issues within the school. There have, however, been some far more exciting examples of involving learners in issues that affect them and in particular their learning. Some examples of these approaches are:

- Having a school improvement team made up of learners.
- Lesson observations carried out by learners. (If staff find this threatening, starting with an appreciative enquiry approach to feedback, discussed later, is a good way to begin.)
- Consultation evenings between parent, teacher and the learner, which are chaired by the learner.
- A school environmental team formed by learners, making recommendations, in order that the school can operate in a more sustainable way.

The schools that use pupil voice in this way are not playing lip service to the concept but involving learners in real issues and giving them real influence in improving the school. Getting feedback from learners is essential if schools are serious about improving learning and indeed Hattie (2008) in his book ' Visible learning' argues that feedback from learners is *the* most important type of feedback. As the Head you will have the opportunity of making this a priority for your school and modelling getting feedback from children for all your staff.

Of course not all learners are always in the frame of mind to learn and dealing with behaviour issues is an essential part of what you have to do. This is even truer now, given the focus on behaviour in the Ofsted framework. However, avoiding being the person who deals with all the behaviour issues is also essential and it is important not to drift unwittingly into this position. Dealing with antisocial or disruptive behaviour can become a rather negative part of the role of both teacher and Headteacher but this need not be so. Many Local Authorities, for example Hampshire Children's Services, have pioneered the Rights Respect and Responsibilities approach within schools and this turns the process of achieving good behaviour more into a 'learning together' process rather than a 'done to' process. I have worked with a number of the schools involved in this development and have been impressed with the effective and yet more positive framework it provides for dealing with behaviour issues. It is based on the United Nations Convention on the rights of the child. Information about this is readily available on the internet. A Rights Respecting School, not only teaches about children's rights, but models rights and responsibilities in all relationships. The structure and back up materials available help develop a consistent approach from staff to behaviour issues and has the potential to help align how parents deal with problems with the approach used by the school. Part of the commitment to this requires the school to inform and engage parents in what the school is trying to achieve. This is often done through information meetings but then reinforced at consultation evenings etc. Parents are encouraged to use the same language that the school will be using when dealing with behaviour issues i.e. rights, respect and responsibilities language. This more positive approach is also very effective in helping learners with behavioural issues to see the implications for themselves and others of their behaviour. This partnership approach can also serve as a way of involving parents more in the learning of their children.

The Government behaviour advisor Charlie Taylor, has recently produced a behaviour checklist for Headteachers and teachers. The list, which contains, a lot of sensible advice, is available on the Department for Education web site at www.education.gov.uk/getting-the-simple-things-right-charlie-taylors-behaviour-checklist

The key point in the checklist is the need to establish *absolute* clarity about the expected standards of pupil behaviour. Much of what follows, for example setting up a tariff of sanctions and rewards and to use them consistently, becomes much easier if this clarity exists.

In conclusion, the really inspirational Headteachers I have worked with are relentless in their pursuit of improving learning. They are themselves learners and take calculated risks, admitting mistakes when they occur, but are always looking for ways to do things better. The research carried out by the Sutton Trust (Improving the impact of teachers on pupil achievement in the UK published in 2011) shows that undoubtedly the best way of improving standards is to work with your teachers because teachers make such an incredible difference, far greater than any other area you might concentrate on as a Headteacher.

Key points
Maintain your credibility in terms of learning.
Model and discuss good learning.
Develop an ethos within which mentoring and coaching thrive.

Further reading:
Southworth G, (2005) *The essentials of school leadership.* Sage Publications Ltd

Leithwood K, Jantzi D, Steinbach R, (1999) *Changing Leadership for Changing Times.* Open University 1

Collins R, (2014). *Skills for the 21st Century: Teaching higher-order thinking* Curriculum & Leadership Journal, curriculum.edu.au

Fisher R, (1998). *Thinking about thinking: Developing meta-cognition in children*
Published by Early Child Development and Care, Taylor & Francis

CHAPTER 5

Building Capacity

• • •

*'Learn from the mistakes of others. You can't live
long enough to make them all yourself'*

ELEANOR ROOSEVELT

INCREASING THE CAPACITY OF THE school to improve is one of the key tasks for school leaders and is recognised as such in its importance in Ofsted inspections. I have worked with a number of schools to try and develop the concept of a Professional Learning Community in order to build capacity for improvement. A lot has been written in recent times about Professional Learning Communities and there is much research available in this area. The model I have used when working with schools, which is my own and therefore is not researched based, is shown below.

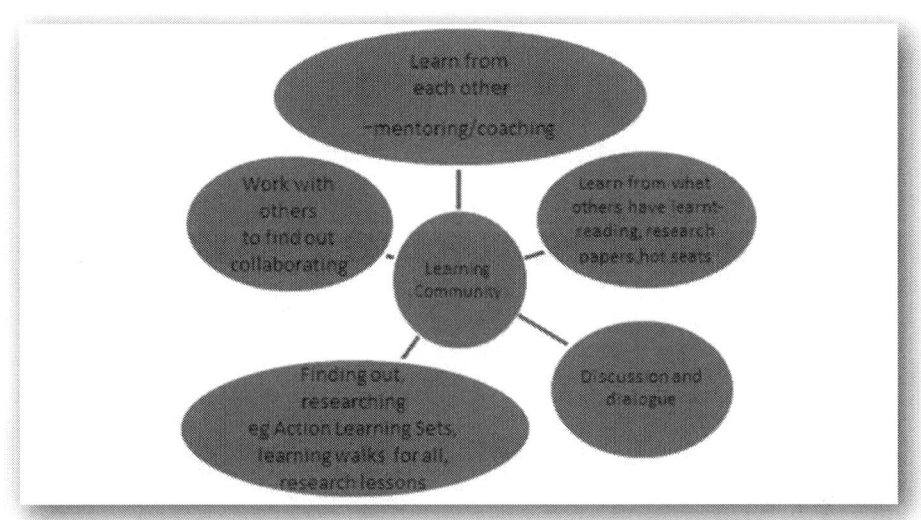

Fig 16 Model of a Professional Learning Community

NCTL has published a number of useful booklets about Professional Learning Communities on their website, many authored by Louise Stoll. One of these booklets contains a helpful list of characteristics observed in effective Learning Communities which is shown below. All of these are implicit in the five strands of the model above.

- Shared values and vision
- Collective responsibility for pupils' learning
- Collaboration focussed on learning
- Group as well as individual learning
- Reflective professional enquiry
- Openness, networks and partnership
- Inclusive membership
- Mutual trust, respect and support

By far the most effective of the five strands for building capacity is to use mentoring and coaching to build the skills of the staff within the school.

The evidence for coaching

The work of Joyce and Showers (1998) shows that if you send a teacher on a course where new approaches are presented by workshop or reading you will have only a very small chance of the teacher changing practice (approximately a 5% chance of changing practice). Following this up, with the chance to model and practise the new approach in a non-threatening situation and get feedback will increase the chances of a change in practice (approximately 30% chance of changing practice), but the really powerful tool is to use coaching where the chances of a change in practice are vastly increased (potentially 90% chance of achieving a change in practice depending on how effective the coach is and how long the coach works with the person being coached). Thus coaching is an essential element of effective professional development.

Mentoring is especially useful for young or new staff and the research around mentoring is mostly positive citing benefits such as 'helping staff to hit the ground running', 'increasing confidence' and 'improved problem solving'. However, there are some downsides. Mentoring is a deficit model in that the mentor is usually placed in the position of the one who knows most and the mentee as the one who needs to ask. Mentoring can also erode confidence if it goes on for too long and the mentee comes to depend too much on the support of the mentor. Coaching, on the other hand, is not inherently a deficit model although some schools fall into the trap of setting it up as a deficit model by immediately targeting coaching at their weakest staff. Everybody can potentially benefit from coaching and if we look at fields where coaching is well developed, such as in sport and industry, the more successful you are the better the coaching you get.

Interestingly, Drucker (2002) talks of the gap between the best and the average performance in an organisation being a constant, but he makes the point that it is easier to raise performance at the top than the middle (in other words, if you make your best staff better the rest will follow). I think there is a lot of merit in focussing coaching on developing strengths and this reinforces the need to avoid just trying to coach the weakest staff. Some schools have adopted a policy within performance management in which staff choose a strength to develop as well as an area they need to address in terms of their practice. Unlike mentoring which consists often of giving advice and answers, coaching is almost the opposite process where the coach works to help the person come up with their own answers. The skills involved in coaching are again focussed on good questioning and active listening as well as the ability to develop empathy and be open minded. The process is intrinsically more challenging than mentoring and offers the opportunity for personal growth for the person being supported. However, coaching is counter-intuitive for some staff and it is advisable that staff who act as coaches have undergone training and skill development activities.

COACHING MODELS

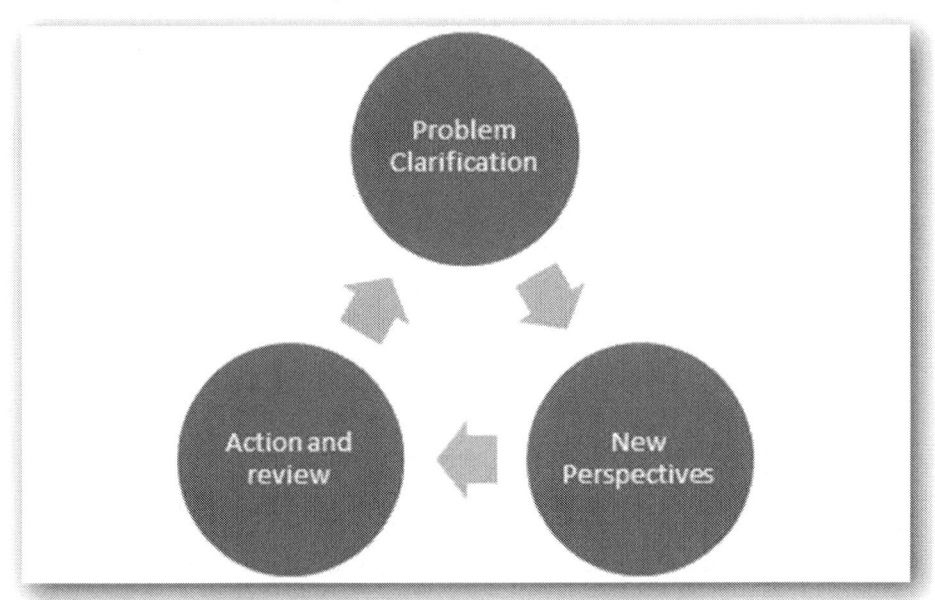

Fig. 17 Processes for effective coaching

When most of us face a problem the process we go through in looking for a solution is to consider similar problems we have had, think about what we did and what resulted and then decide what to do. All these processes are based in the past and are very limiting. What a coach does is to try and help the person see new opportunities by getting them to look at the problem from different and new perspectives. This is illustrated in the cycle above.

However there are a number of other coaching models. The most widely used in education is probably the GROW model developed by Sir John Whitmore (1984). There are four stages in this model:

G - goal identification
R - current reality
O – opportunities
W – willingness to act.

Typically in a GROW coaching session the coach begins by using listening and questioning skills to establish the outcome the person being coached would be happy with. This is essential because if the coach does not do this he or she may well make inaccurate assumptions about the desired outcome. The coach would then explore the current situation and the opportunities for action. Finally after the person being coached has chosen the new action they want to pursue the coach would discuss barriers as well as timescales for the new strategy.

Some schools find it useful to introduce coaching to staff through a model but there are potential problems. The coaching can become very formulaic and the model assumes that the person being coached will be aware of the goal when they start and that the coaching process is linear. Often these assumptions do not match reality. For example, it will often be the case that the person will, in fact, start with the symptoms of a problem rather than the core issue which they may not have yet identified. In this situation they are not immediately aware of the goal they want to achieve. Having said this, in trying to develop a coaching culture, the model provides a useful starting point.

The focus of coaching does not have to be a problem and staff are sometimes much more willing to engage in coaching activities that do not start with a problem. For example, two colleagues can have a coaching conversation about a recent successful lesson. The job of the one acting as the coach is to listen and ask some insightful questions which will help the teacher take some deeper learning from this successful lesson into their future planning. This is an activity I have used successfully in a number of schools as a way of engaging staff in coaching activities.

When to coach and when to mentor

In terms of effectively supporting staff to build their coaching skills the key issue is to know when to coach and when to mentor. If we try to mentor when coaching is needed almost inevitably the mentoring will fail.

The following diagram is helpful in establishing when to coach and when to mentor.

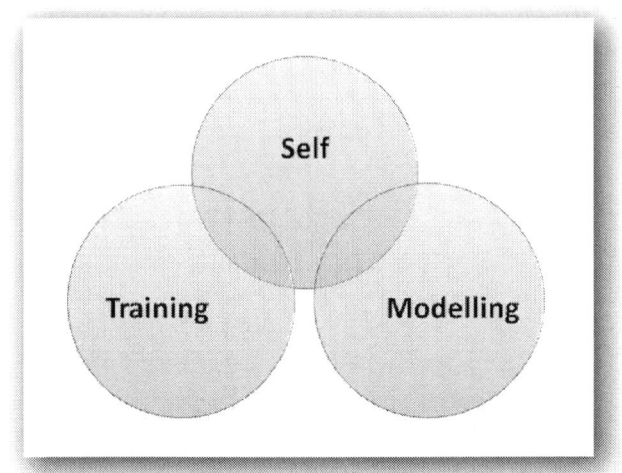

Fig. 18 When to Coach and when to mentor.

    Whenever a person carries out a role, the way in which they carry out the role is influenced by three domains. First, any training they have received which affects the way they carry out the role, secondly any modelling they have experienced that affects how they carry out the role and thirdly their own personality and life experience and DNA which will have an effect on how they carry out the role. This last area is labelled Self. The relative importance of the three influences varies from one role to another. For somebody working on a supermarket checkout the training and modelling areas would be very influential. They might receive training perhaps on a dummy checkout and then go on to watch somebody modelling the work on a check-out and both these would have a large influence on how they did the job. Once fully trained and working, however, the Self segment would play quite a small role since social interactions are short and often perfunctory on a supermarket checkout. If there were problems while working at the check-out usually the person would indicate this to a supervisor, and the supervisor would come to help them and would mentor them by providing a solution.

Mentoring is the first strategy to try if the problem is perceived to be a matter of lack of training or modelling. However, if the issue is related to the Self segment, for example to do with relationships, then mentoring will often not be appropriate since it would be very difficult to give another person answers in this area where we may have had completely different experiences and personalities.

In teaching, the Self component is very large compared to the training and modelling components and therefore the potential for mentoring is much reduced. If you have watched lots of different teachers teach you can see how much of what they do depends on their personality. In my experience often in schools we have the balance between coaching and mentoring wrong and too much mentoring goes on. Often, therefore, we end up mentoring when we should be coaching. Consider for example two Newly Qualified Teachers (NQTs). One is coping very well but perhaps having a problem with a couple of learners. Usually we would mentor in this case and offer some advice perhaps in terms of classroom management or a more differentiated approach to learning. This would probably work because the issue often lies in the training or modelling area. However, if we had an NQT who was having problems with many of the learners or classes they taught we tend to adopt the same strategy and offer advice. This normally fails and they come back for help and they are often offered yet more advice. This is because the problem is much more likely to be tied up with their personality or the way they interact with the learners i.e. in the Self area, and we might be much more effective by coaching them. They could then come up with their own approaches to help tackle the issue. Given the potential power of coaching it is no wonder that Goleman (2004), identifies the coaching leadership style as the one that most effective in building capacity and improving standards.

USING EDUCATIONAL RESEARCH – MAKING TEACHING AN EVIDENCE-BASED PROFESSION

Another aspect of a Professional Learning Community is learning from what others have learnt. Education is increasingly an evidenced-based profession and there is a wealth of useful research which schools have access to if they seek it out. This could be as simple as using articles from *The Times Educational Supplement* or more formal research papers about learning and leadership from an educational data base such as Education Resources Information Centre (ERIC can be found at www.eric.ed.gov). You, as Head, can model the use of research as a resource for improving learning for your staff. For example, one Headteacher I worked with would, together with members of the leadership team, often photocopy articles and put them in staff pigeon holes and then spend a short time at the next staff meeting discussing any implications for practice. Middle leaders were encouraged to do the same with their teams. This models learning for the staff in a very powerful way and helps staff to see the importance of continuing professional learning.

Things that work in other schools, however, still have to be shown to work in your school. The people working in schools are unique and therefore each school is unique. Thus we have to 'see if it works here' by trying it out. This 'finding out' branch of the Professional Learning Community could also involve activities such as forming action-learning groups within the school to look at learning issues which are felt to be a priority.

Action-learning sets, research lesson and learning walks

Action-learning sets are groups whose participants use a combination of reflection and action to improve performance. Learners acquire knowledge through their actual actions rather than through traditional instruction. Action-learning enables each person to reflect on and review the action they have taken and the learning points arising. This then guides future action and improved performance.

Action-learning sets are a powerful tool for developing reflective and more effective practitioners and can become the research and development engine within the school. They can often also encourage staff to take their learning further, for example, by registering for a M.Ed. or similar qualification. Action-learning sets also enable participants to learn from each other and build a strong support network within the school or across schools.

The internet provides details of other useful tools for supporting research in schools. We have already mentioned Research lessons and Blink (National Educational Trust website 'What is Blink?') provides a protocol for learning walks which will maximise the learning from walking your own school or when visiting a colleague's school

Working with others

Another aspect of the Professional Learning Community embraces networking and working with other organisations. This is a broad area and would encompass everything from working with groups within the community, including parents, to strategic alliances with other schools in order to work on specific issues. Some of these schools will be within your own academy chain. David Hargreaves in his paper 'Creating a self-improving schools system '(available on the DFE website) points the way to the importance of schools working together in the education system of the 21st century. Hargreaves talks of 'Co-operation ceasing to be the opposite of competition'. The Academies movement provide some good examples of how this can be done. As schools begin to consider and move to academy status the potential for networking should be one of the considerations. No matter how effective a school is it will always benefit on occasion by working and learning from others. Too often, however, the networks that Headteachers inherit when they join a school are sometimes characterised by competition between the members and a lack of trust and sharing. If this is the case their value really needs to be questioned. Contrast this with a group of schools who freely choose to work and share everything together which is an incredibly powerful tool for professional learning and school improvement. Successful Headteachers in the current educational climate have to become good networkers and to be able to build effective support systems from their relationships with other Heads. The skills needed for good networking are, I believe, related to those of being a good entrepreneur: the ability to make connections between new and old knowledge, the ability to innovate, the ability to see and take opportunities and the ability to attract resources. The links between Hargreaves' (2012) model for self-improving schools is shown below.

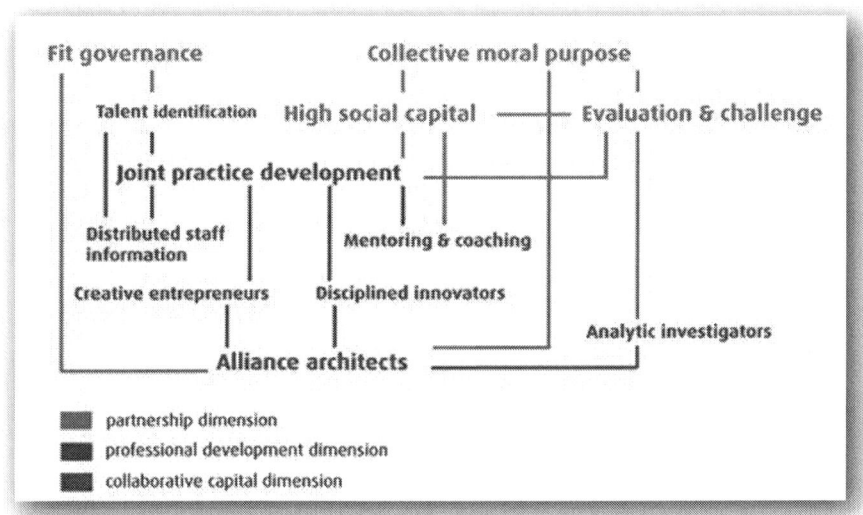

```
Fit governance              Collective moral purpose
     |                              |         |
  Talent identification   High social capital ——— Evaluation & challenge
     |                              |         |
  Joint practice development ———————————————————
     |                              |
  Distributed staff            Mentoring & coaching
  information                       |
  Creative entrepreneurs      Disciplined innovators
              |                     |
              Alliance architects              Analytic investigators

■ partnership dimension
■ professional development dimension
■ collaborative capital dimension
```

Fig. 19 Hargreaves model of self improving school system

Building a Professional Learning Community within your school is a really important task and should be given a high priority within the SLT.

RECRUITING THE RIGHT STAFF.
Another important aspect of building school capacity will be your role in recruitment. I have worked with some Headteachers who are particularly accomplished in recruiting good staff and this not only helps establish a school as outstanding but also helps sustain it as such. How do they

manage to do it? A few observations I would make having seen them in action would be:

- Don't appoint because you are desperate to do so - you will probably have many years to regret this!
- Appoint people who are likely to get promoted and perhaps move on. Although this can cause you problems in terms of replacing them in the long run it is a more effective approach.
- Don't look for clones. Covey (1989) mentions the importance of synergy in his book 'The seven habits of highly effective people'. He defines this as ability to work with and recognise the strengths of people who are different from you.
- As well as spending time establishing that the person you appoint is a good teacher also spend time establishing what they really believe about education and ensure this is compatible with the school ethos.
- Put a high value on intelligence.
- During lesson observations watch the body language of the teacher and interactions with the students.
- Don't make appointments only on the basis of good references; make sure you see all the strengths mentioned.
- If you use a variety of activities during the selection process think very carefully about how they should be weighted in terms of the final decision.

I don't offer these suggestions as blueprint for good appointments merely as observations on the strategies used by those whom I have worked with who seemed to be good at what is a difficult but crucial task. Having made a good appointment it is now important to ensure a successful induction into the new post. One important element of induction that is often missed out is to take new staff through some of the thinking and dialogue about improving teaching and learning that has taken place over recent times in the school so that they can align and contribute in a positive way more quickly. Taking new staff through the 'thinking at this school' is as important as making them familiar with policies, systems and structures.

BUILDING EFFECTIVE TEAMS

Another important aspect of capacity building is the extent to which you can build effective teams. The most effective Heads form their staff into powerful teams that support, protect and improve the school. However, sometimes the Middle Leaders that you inherit as a Headteacher have had little leadership training and in fact, by and large, tend to manage their teams rather than lead them. This can also be true of the members of the SLT that lead teams within the school. However, if we want to focus on school improvement, managing the current situation efficiently is not going to be enough and we need Middle Leaders not Middle Managers. Using the language of leadership i.e. subject leaders, numeracy leader, Senior Leadership Team rather than Senior Management Team etc, is one essential way to reinforce this message. Providing some on-going development programme for Middle Leaders is also an important step to developing effective teams. The National College of Teaching and Leadership 'National Professional Qualification for Middle Leaders' programme would be an excellent starting point or alternatively the SLT could design a customised programme. Access to this type of on-going programme again models the fact that staff are working in a learning organisation.

TEAM EFFECTIVENESS.

There is a large body of knowledge about team effectiveness so I shall just concentrate on the aspects of the research available that I have experience of using and which I know has proved useful in a number of schools. This is the Beckhard (1972) model for team effectiveness shown in the figure below.

Fig. 20 Beckhard's model

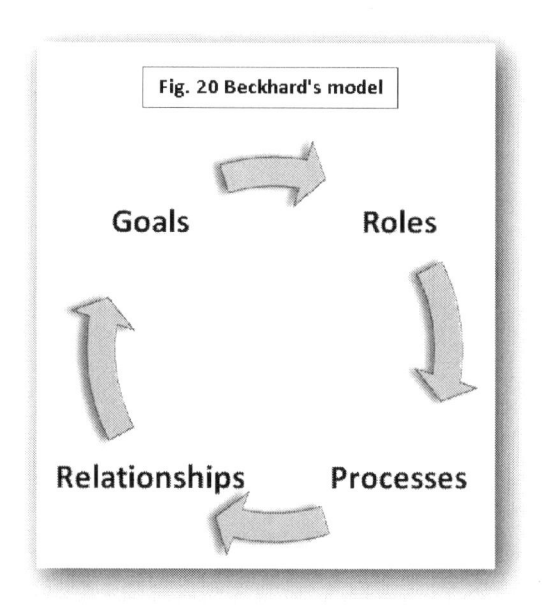

Goals → Roles → Processes → Relationships → Goals

The model is deceptively simple. In essence it shows that effective teams are clear about their goals, everybody in the team understands the role they need to play in order to reach the goals, people can engage effectively in the processes designed to help to reach the goals and this in turn builds good relationships. The goals need to be articulated in a way that is meaningful to the everyday work of those in the school. If the goals are not clear then people cannot play a full role in achieving them. It is easy to fall into the trap of setting a goal without explaining clearly what the goal looks like in terms of the everyday life of the school. For example, I once worked with a leadership team whose stated goal was to promote independent learning. However, when I asked them what independent learning was there was a debate for an hour and a half! Leaders of teams really need to hammer out what the goals they want to achieve really look like if they are not to confuse staff.

Follow up research on the Beckhard model looked at dysfunctionality in teams, and found that very often people would describe the dysfunctionality in terms of relationships. 'The problem with my team is Fred!' However, when the dysfunctionality was analysed it was often just a symptom of poorly defined goals. If I am a member of a team with poorly defined goals then I can't play a full role in achieving them and I can't play a full part in processes set up to achieve the goals. The frustration that follows from this situation will often impact negatively on relationships. The lesson from Beckhard's work is that all leaders within the school must develop clear meaningful goals for their teams covering both the long and short term, if they are to be effective. In many ways you cannot be too explicit.

What do we know about effective teams?

If we look at the observational research on effective teams we get a list of characteristics like the one below.

- Have a shared understanding of the vision and tasks that flow from the vision
- The skills of the team meet the needs of the organisation
- The team members are loyal to each other and respect each other's contribution
- Members work on problems together
- The team adapts and is positive about change
- The team is aware of its development needs
- New members are inducted carefully
- The team takes calculated risks
- The team prioritises and shares leadership
- Communications within the team are good and people can express their opinions
- The team always looks to improve its performance
- The members of the team lead by example

This type of audit is interesting in what it tells us about effective teams but can also provide a useful framework for a team to review its effectiveness periodically. I have used similar lists to help SLTs reflect on their performance and develop a programme for improved working since, however good they may be as a team, they can always improve.

We also know from the work of Roberts (1990) on highly effective teams that getting feedback on the team's performance is very important. In order to do this effectively the purpose of the team must be clearly understood by those giving feedback. Unfortunately, because many of the teams that work in schools have met in the same way for many years, it is often the case that the members of a team have never actually discussed why they meet! If this is the case the value of any feedback about team performance is obviously greatly reduced. Assuming this is not the scenario, feedback can be gathered simply from members of the team by using the 'what went well, even better if' technique. This method of getting feedback is widely used by NCSL and the language of 'even better if' encourages people to give honest feedback.

CONCEPTUAL MODEL OF AN EFFECTIVE TEAM.

One of the observations in the list above is that the skills of the team match its purpose. It is therefore useful to have some sort of framework within which to carry out a skills audit within the team. A number of such frameworks exist and I have worked with some teams that drew up their own.

Perhaps the most widely used, however, would be the framework developed by Meredith Belbin (1981)

Belbin's work led to a conceptual model of an effective team which had the following skill set:

- Plant, creative, solves difficult problems
- Co-ordinator, clarifies goals, promotes decision-making
- Monitor, Evaluator
- Implementer, turns ideas in practical action

- Completer Finisher
- Resource Investigator, enthusiastic, explores opportunities
- Shaper, challenges
- Teamworker, co-operative builds consensus
- Specialist, provides knowledge and skills in rare supply

(Members of the team can complete a questionnaire which will indicate their strongest skills within the team.)

These are all skills that are permanently needed but there is also a non-permanent member of the team that Belbin calls the specialist. This extra person was needed because Belbin felt that no team ever had all the specialist knowledge it needed and so at times it would need to work with others from outside the team in order to get the specialist knowledge it needed. This is interesting when we think of teams in schools which very often have fixed membership and do not have a culture of recognising when they need specialist support to help do their work effectively. In some of the most effective SLTs I have worked with they often invite people to join the team and 'Hot Seat' in order to use their expertise. 'Hot Seating', where a specialist comes along and just answers questions is often more effective than inviting them along to give a presentation. 'Hot Seats' ensure that the process addresses your learning agenda.

There are a number of potential advantages in working with a conceptual model such as this. If you carry out a skills audit it helps recognise the leadership skills of all members of the team. If the team leader uses these skills within the team e.g. 'Tim, you are our shaper - anything we are missing here……?' 'Jane, you are our plant - any new approaches you can see?' this provides a potential way to distribute leadership within the team and grow leadership capacity. The Belbin model can also be used as part of a recruitment process where identifying a particular skill set is a high priority. The other advantage of carrying out a Belbin skills audit of your team is that it enables you to work more effectively with both your strengths and weaknesses. The emotional intelligence link, outlined by Goleman (1998), between self-awareness and self-management for effective individuals is equally valid for teams. Thus, for example, if a team finds itself low on Plant then it could bring someone more creative in to help when dealing with an intractable problem that requires some creativity, or alternatively it could ensure that a member of the team thoroughly researches the options, what others may have done in similar situations etc., and brings this research to the meeting. Thus, compensating strategies can be developed to make the team more effective.

Project management teams

Another method of distributing leadership more widely in order to build leadership capacity and give staff leadership experience is the use of project management teams. Many of the teams within schools are standing teams with fixed membership and power structures. Project Management Teams offer the opportunity for more flexibility in that those who perhaps haven't yet led a team or played a major role in a team can be given the chance to take on some more responsibility. Project Management Groups can also be very effective for problem solving since they make better use of talent and creativity. Such teams are usually given a fixed amount of time in which to work and can be an effective mechanism for distributing leadership. One issue with Project Management Teams is that you have to be careful to ensure good communication in all directions in terms of what the team is doing as the normal channels of communication will not have been set up to include the team.

Change teams are examples of the type of Project Management Teams schools have used. These often involve representatives from a number of stakeholder groups and were used for example by many schools when implementing workforce reform. However, they have potential to be used in many other scenarios especially when a greater diversity of experience and knowledge is beneficial.

The Senior Leadership Team

The most important team in all schools is the Senior Leadership Team. In recent years the size of these teams has grown often in an attempt to distribute leadership within schools. For most Headteachers the SLT is crucial to their work within the school. The members of the team are often the closest to you personally and provide support in what is a notoriously lonely job. It is important, however, that this support really adds value to the work of the Headteacher and does not turn into an opportunity for mutual sympathy. Really good SLTs will challenge your thinking by asking questions which add value to the dialogue about learning and change. The strongest teams are self-evaluative and constantly look to improve. In order to get the sort of honesty and openness needed to achieve this you need to model these behaviours and reinforce them positively when you see others practising them. When they work well together the SLT and the Head can provide a sounding and test board for each other in carrying out their responsibilities.

Developing a common language of leadership amongst the team is also important in terms of developing understanding of leadership and the effectiveness of the team. The use of process tools such as the Beckhard change equation and others explained throughout the book help develop transparency and clarity about how the team works. This in turn develops trust and accountability as well as developing a shared language of leadership.

Mutual coaching within the team, based on leadership skills, is also an effective way of building leadership capacity and developing a common understanding of leadership. The team will need to meet regularly in order to really be a team and will need to manage their time so that there is an appropriate balance between the urgent and the important. The ethos at meetings needs to be solution-focussed rather than problem-focussed. Again, if you model this, the rest of the team and the staff will often follow your lead.

When I have looked at how successful teams are built in industry one of the things that has struck me is that, in general, they are much more explicit about the expected behaviours and responsibilities of team members. I think this is actually a very positive thing to do in order to ensure teams are effective. An example of this explicitness in terms of team behaviours is shown below, and is taken from a commercial company website. Such a protocol can of course quickly be generated by the members of any team. The leader would, however, in either case have to ensure the protocol was followed and manage situations where staff strayed from it, if it is to be useful.

Positive team behaviours:

Clarifying behaviour
Supporting behaviour
Initiating behaviour
Mediating behaviour
Energising behaviour
Regulating behaviour

Negative team behaviours:

Dominating behaviour
Blocking behaviour
Rambling behaviour
Withdrawing behaviour

Dealing with underperformance

However good the support and development systems within a school there will be some occasions when a member of staff's performance falls short of what is acceptable. These are never easy situations to deal with but it is essential that they are not put off. When going through the capability process I think it is helpful for the Headteacher to go into role and just keep in mind throughout that the needs of the children are paramount to your purpose.

There is plenty of support and advice available to Headteachers engaged in the process and it is important to access this. The Performance Management arrangements (September 2012) offer the opportunity of a faster capability process and many Headteachers will welcome this.

Growing your own leaders.

All Headteachers are responsible for succession planning within their school and an important part of this is the development of leadership capacity in others. Just as recruitment of staff is a key issue for all Headteachers the recruitment and development of leaders is of equal importance. There is a lot of research about this area of leadership and the following is a summary of good practice for potential leaders you might want to bring on.

- Let them interact with current leaders. (shadow, work together)
- Teach them to network and give them the opportunity to.
- Give them a little power. Can be task-based to avoid clashes of responsibility.
- Be a mentor.
- Be clear about your beliefs about leadership
- Get them a coach
- Give them feedback about their leadership skills.
- Invest in training and development.
- Encourage and support initiative.
- Be a role model

Key points
Coach and develop other leaders in the school
Only appoint the best. Only the best is good enough for your children!
Work with team leaders to help them make their teams effective

FURTHER READING:

Senge P, (1990). *The fifth discipline* Publisher : Doubleday/Currency. ISBN 0385260946

Hargreaves A, Fink D, (2003) *Sustaining Leadership* In b. Davies B & West-Burnham J (eds)

Handbook of Leadership and Management, Pearson

Harkins P, (2006) *10 Leadership Techniques for Building High-Performing Teams*

Linkage

CHAPTER 6

Increasing your personal effectiveness

• • •

'A leader is a dealer in hope'

Napoleon Bonaparte

In my work with Headteachers I have often found myself supporting them in their efforts to become more personally effective as leaders. Increasing your personal effectiveness involves a focus on you and your skills rather than all the tasks and problems you face. Much of the training we tend to do in education is very much context based, 'learning about' rather than learning 'how to'. Fortunately this is beginning to change and the new NPQH model does make personal effectiveness a focus for development of trainee Headteachers. Reflecting on, and adopting strategies to improve your personal effectiveness is a characteristic of the best leaders. Changing behaviours and habits is by no means easy though. However, if you can get better at listening, questioning or some other relevant skill you will get the benefit of this improvement throughout your career so the potential rewards are great.

STRENGTHS AND AREAS FOR DEVELOPMENT.

One of the easiest ways to improve personal effectiveness is first of all to concentrate on your strengths and build on them. Leaders often take their strengths for granted but regularly reflecting on them and how you could make more use of them as a leader is always a useful process. Audit tools are a useful starting place when looking at which area of personal effectiveness to work on. I have successfully used the National Standards for School Leadership for this purpose and an emotional literacy audit. Emotional Intelligence (EI) audits are available on the internet and EI is an increasing focus within Headteacher appointments. Choosing an audit tool provides a framework for reflecting on the areas in which you want to develop your skills as a leader.

Once a focus or area of personal effectiveness has been decided on, the internet will provide a ready source of information on the area you have chosen. Sites such as *Businessballs* (www.businessballs.com) is an excellent free online learning resource for leaders, the DFE website, Sutton Trust website as well as education data bases such as ERIC are examples of where information can be found. Often within a few hits it is possible to pick up a lot of useful information about a particular skill or ability and how to develop it. Having achieved a greater understanding of the area you are interested in the hard part is how to turn this knowledge into a new behaviour. The work of Boyatzis (1999) on self-directed learning provides some useful support in this area. Boyatzis' model is shown below:

The First Discovery
- My ideal self
- Who do I want to be?

The Second Discovery
- My real self
- Who am I?
- What are my strengths and gaps?

The Third Discovery
- - My learning agenda
- - How can I build on my strengths while reducing my gap?

The Fourth Discovery
- - Experimenting with new behaviours, thoughts and feelings to the point of mastery
- - What actions do I need to take?

The Fifth Discovery
- - Developing trusting relationships that help, support and encourage each step in the process
- - Who can help me?

Fig. 21 Boyatzis model.

The model encourages leaders to reflect on what sort of leader they want to be and what are their current strengths and areas for development. Step four, practising until mastery, is very important so that you give yourself the chance to improve in small steps which will help you embed the change in behaviour rather than going for immediate transformation. You are much more likely to persevere with the practising of the new behaviour if you are working with somebody who is aware of what you are trying to do, as indicated in step 5, and with whom you can discuss progress or get some feedback. This approach of working with somebody who is aware of your target in order to increase your commitment to change is used very effectively in other organisations such as Weightwatchers and Alcoholics Anonymous.

WORKING WITH A COACH.

Another approach to improving personal effectiveness would be to work with a coach. The current model of NPQH offers trainee Headteachers this opportunity. I believe working with a coach is almost always beneficial and it is good to see that the opportunity to work with a Professional

Partner (coach/mentor) is now part of the Induction of new Headteachers. I believe all Heads should have access to a trained mentor/coach. Some time ago I carried out two evaluations of Headteacher induction as part of work I did with NCTL and coaching was by far the most valued part of the induction programmes. Working with a coach has the added advantage of helping you to develop your own coaching skills.

TIME MANAGEMENT.

An area that repeatedly comes up when working with leaders to improve their personal effectiveness is time management. Headteachers are incredibly busy people with wide areas of responsibility and managing their time is crucially important to their effectiveness. Many of the techniques we have already covered will have a positive effect on time management, for example, having an effective approach to accountability will make it less likely that the Head ends up doing other people's jobs, which happens more frequently than it should. Similarly, building leadership capacity will increase the number of people the Headteacher can turn to for support. One useful discipline however, is to regularly reflect on how you spend your time as a leader and how better to manage it. The following questions can aid this process:

What must I stop doing by diplomatically rejecting? e.g. unplanned interruptions, apparent emergencies and off loads from others.

What must I resist and then cease doing? e.g. unnecessary emails, reading irrelevant materials, attending meetings which are not useful.

The list of time-stealers shown below is useful in helping you to focus on the areas you need to manage more effectively.

- Sitting in front of the computer-move it to another desk!
- Interruptions – telephone
- Interruptions - personal visitors
- Meetings
- Tasks you should have delegated

- Procrastination and indecision
- Acting with incomplete information
- Dealing with team members
- Crisis management (fire fighting)
- Unclear communication
- Inadequate technical knowledge
- Unclear objectives and priorities
- Lack of planning
- Stress and fatigue
- Inability to say "No"

It is also worth considering activities which don't take a lot of time but give a high return.

There are some high profile times of the day when the Headteacher can ensure that he or she is seen by all staff, learners or parents. An example would be gate duty or being around at lunch time. These times are valuable in terms of building an ethos of leadership where the Headteacher is seen to be involved in the life of the school rather than a remote figure in an office.

Effective delegation

As we have mentioned building leadership capacity will increase the pool of people who can share the leadership of the school. Delegation is an important part of achieving this and it is worth spending some time thinking about how to ensure that when you delegate to staff, you do so effectively. Many Heads I have worked with often complain that they can't delegate things because staff continually keep checking with them to ensure they are doing the right thing and it is almost quicker to do the job yourself. This is often symptomatic of not making it clear to staff the level of authority they have in order to carry out the task you have given them. Often leaders are much better at delegating tasks than at delegating the authority to do them. In order to effectively empower a member of staff to carry out a task the first step is to brief them thoroughly about the area of responsibility you are giving them and the things you want them to take into consideration etc. Taking the time to be as explicit as possible about this saves time later. You also need to be explicit with them, and with any other staff involved, about the authority you are giving them in order to carry out the task. Finally you need to ensure that you build in some time to hold them to account for what they do. If any of these elements are missing empowerment is only partial and continual checking is sometimes an indicator of this. Delegation always involves an element of letting go and overcoming the temptation to micromanage which is at the root of many time management issues. It is also wise to avoid delegating the things you don't like doing as this quickly becomes recognised as 'dumping'. To whom and what to delegate is a key part of delegation. The temptation is often to give your best people your most difficult problems to tackle but a better approach is sometimes to give them tasks related to your greatest opportunities for improvement.

Think of empowerment as a tripod – if one leg is missing it doesn't work!

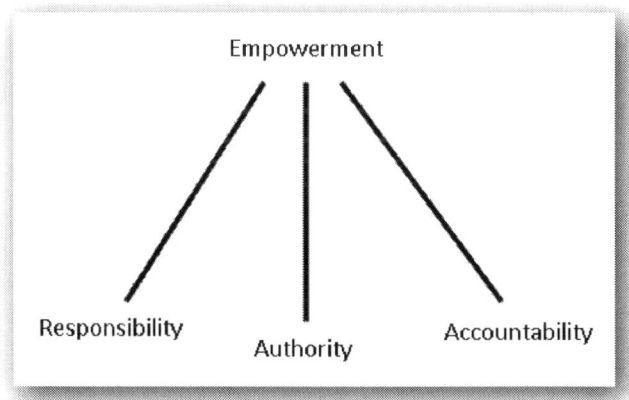

Fig. 22 Empowerment diagram

We tend to be good in schools at giving people responsibility but without the authority to carry things out this leads to frustration for the person we have delegated the task to. If we give authority but without checking through accountability systems we run the risk of the person going off in a direction we are not happy with. Good delegation is a fine balance between these things but is essential not only because of its impact on time management but on the leadership development of staff. Jim Collins (2001) gives some good advice on delegation when he says get your best people to work on your greatest opportunities not your biggest problems.

The importance of being a listening leader

Two of the most useful skills in terms of personal effectiveness are the ability to actively listen and to ask good questions. We have seen previously that these skills are important when holding people to account and when coaching. The truth is, however, they are important in almost all aspects of leadership. Stephen Covey (1989) talks of effective people, seeking to understand, and then to be understood. This involves having good active listening skills. The danger is that as a leader if you don't take the time to listen you will end up making more assumptions and many of these will be wrong!

Unfortunately, sometimes leaders are not naturally good listeners because they are used to listening for influence. This is why they often interrupt, relate what is being said to their own experience and interpret what is being said in terms of its effect on them. This type of listening is often described as 'listening to self'. Developing listening skills is thus often something that Headteachers want and need to work on, and one of the most successful strategies they can adopt to improve listening skills is to practise not thinking about what you are going to say until the other person has stopped talking. This has the added advantage of getting you used to small periods of silence which is essential to good listening. Another useful activity is to practise some 80:20 conversations where you try to speak for only 20% of the time. It is important to say that 'listening to self' is not always wrong, after all

Headteachers have to be able to influence others, merely that it is not always appropriate. Listening to people properly conveys respect and as Dean Rusk, American Secretary of State, said 'One of the best ways to persuade others is with your ears - by listening to them'. When having difficult conversations it is particularly important that leaders show they are listening since this helps achieve acceptance which is often the best you can hope for when giving somebody a message they don't want to hear. Good questioning is another key leadership skill.

CHALLENGING THROUGH QUESTIONING - 'CHALLENGE THINKING AS PART OF CHANGING PRACTICE'.

Developing questioning skills is an important part of having effective conversations and skilled leaders can learn to criticize by using a questioning in a way which is challenging but not damaging to relationships. Skilled questioning is a high order skill and one that effective leaders continually strive to develop.

As Peter Drucker said in a talk to the Drucker Foundation Advisory Board in 1993 '..the leader of the past was a person who knew how to tell. The leader of the future will be a person who knows how to ask'. However, asking good questions is more easily said than done and you will need to practise this.

In Chapter 1 we looked at how authenticity is linked to the relationship between what we believe, what we say and what we do. When we become leaders, however, we get a fourth layer 'what we do when there are problems in our team'. For example, suppose as a teacher I believe in Assessment for Learning. I also talk very positively to others about it and use it in my classroom. In personal terms I am authentic with regard to AfL. If I am made co-ordinator of AfL, however, and I have a member of my team who really only plays lip service to using AfL and may be negative about it in the staffroom I have to tackle this issue or risk losing my authenticity as a leader in the eyes of my team.

Fig. 23. Authenticity triangle.

The reality for leaders is that they have to find the courage to tackle difficult issues if they are to retain authenticity. Helping Headteachers to find their own way of doing this is often another focus for improving personal effectiveness. This work often involves developing the ability to be assertive when needed. Assertiveness is often considered in a rather negative light but if we think of it as lying between aggressiveness and submissiveness we can see that for leaders it is essential to be able to be assertive when necessary. In general it is far easier to be assertive and get the outcome you want from a difficult situation when you are well prepared for it. This is how staff are trained when they work in situations in which they have to be assertive, for example on a returns counter at a shop or on a complaints telephone line. These staff would be trained in such a way that no matter whatever the problem encountered they would know exactly what their response will be and indeed follow up responses to your response to them. Difficult conversations, for example about underperformance, require the same sort of preparation. The worse possible strategy is to try and put the meeting out of your mind until it's upon you!

When giving somebody a message they don't want to hear it is essential to share with them the evidence on which the decision or conversation is based so that you don't end up trading opinions. It is also useful to outline the downsides for them before they do. This will not only demonstrate that you have thought about it from their point of view but will mean downsides emerge in a slightly less negative way than would be the case if they raised the concerns and so adds less to the adversarial nature of the situation. In preparing for such a meeting you must think of all the likely responses you will get when you give them the message they don't want to hear and have your own responses ready. This will give you added confidence for what is never a pleasant process. The reality is that if you are to be effective as a leader you have to find a way to deal with these difficult conversations. At times you will also need to use official procedures in cases where performance slips below an acceptable level. When approaching capability procedures it is worth remembering that these are support procedures and must be approached as such albeit in the end they can lead to somebody being dismissed. Seeking support from personnel specialists and from your union in these situations is always a good strategy, ducking the issue is not! Putting off difficult conversations can often stop you functioning effectively. Staff involved in receiving hard messages can become upset and try to engage the Headteacher on an emotional level. Even though you may well have sympathy for the person allowing yourself to get engaged emotionally is nearly always a mistake. Sir John Jones talks in his seminars about avoiding getting involved emotionally by starting with 'On a personal level I don't want to have this conversation but on a professional level I think I must.' and I have always found this a very useful and effective approach. Whenever you have to engage in a difficult conversation it is always useful to spend some time reflecting, perhaps with a coach, on what you have learnt from the experience.

Leadership style

There has been a great deal written about the effects of leadership style and the body of research on this topic is huge. For me the most useful and practical research on the subject, and I think currently the most influential research, has been carried out by Goleman (2001).

Goleman identifies six aspects of what he calls Emotionally Intelligent Leadership. These are:

Visionary, sometimes described as Authoritative
Coaching
Affiliative
Democratic
Pacesetting
Commanding

All leaders use elements of each of these styles and each has its value in particular circumstances. For example if a school is in Special Measures then a Commanding style of leadership might be very successful. In other circumstances it may not. The most interesting aspects of Goleman's work, however, are where he looks at the results of using these different leadership styles. This part of his research was carried out with the Hay/McBer group. In summary the results show:

- when a leader is working with staff in Visionary and Coaching mode he or she is building leadership capacity within the organisation and helping to develop other leaders. These modes of EI leadership also have a positive influence on organisational climate.

Pacesetting and Commanding do not build capacity and can have a negative impact on organisational climate. This is interesting in view of the amount of Pacesetting that some Headteachers engineer. Goleman talks about using Pacesetting 'sparingly'. It is not that any of these styles are wrong, merely that is useful to consider the results of using them. Perhaps the most interesting aspect of this is the effect on standards.

Coaching and Visionary are the leadership styles that have the most positive effect on standards. Visionary and Affiliative have the biggest positive effect on commitment to the organisation and Visionary and Coaching have the biggest impact on clarity of purpose. I think these results confirm the importance we have already given to a Headteacher developing a compelling vivid future and developing their own coaching skills through good listening and questioning.

Building Trust

Trust in never easy to define but I think the quote that 'trust is what happens when values and behaviours match up' is useful in clarifying what we mean by trust. Leaders who are personally effective are often ones in whom followers express high levels of trust. Building trust is a key element of success as a leader but there is always tension between levels of monitoring and levels of trust and getting the balance right is never easy. Covey and Merrill (2006) in their book 'The speed of trust' look at leadership behaviours that help to build trust. These are shown in the list below and are a good starting point in terms of how to begin to build and maintain trust in your school.

- Talk Straight
- Demonstrate Respect
- Create Transparency
- Right Wrongs
- Show Loyalty
- Get Better
- Confront Reality
- Clarify Expectations
- Practise Accountability
- Listen First
- Keep Commitments, and
- Extend Trust

The other interesting aspect of Covey and Merrill's findings is that organisations where levels of trust are low are very inefficient. Thus leaders should always be trying to grow trust in order to make their organisations more efficient and effective. They do not advocate ever relinquishing the need to monitor, merely that you need a balance and the direction of travel should be towards greater trust and less monitoring.

Levels of trust within a school are dynamic and sometimes you will need to make building trust more of a priority in terms of how you prioritise your time. This can be especially important at times of rapid change. Indeed, a leader builds trust and cohesiveness simply by keeping people informed. Having in mind some indicators of levels of trust is useful when making these judgements. Examples of such indicators are the number of staff asking questions and contributing at staff meetings, the level of risk taking in the school, even the body language of the staff and the use of humour.

FEEDBACK

One difficult area in terms of increasing personal effectiveness, but one that has to be grasped is that of getting honest feedback about your leadership. This is more difficult than it might seem because staff will often give you the feedback they think you want to hear.

The Johari Window developed by Luft and Ingham (1950) shows how important it is to get feedback.

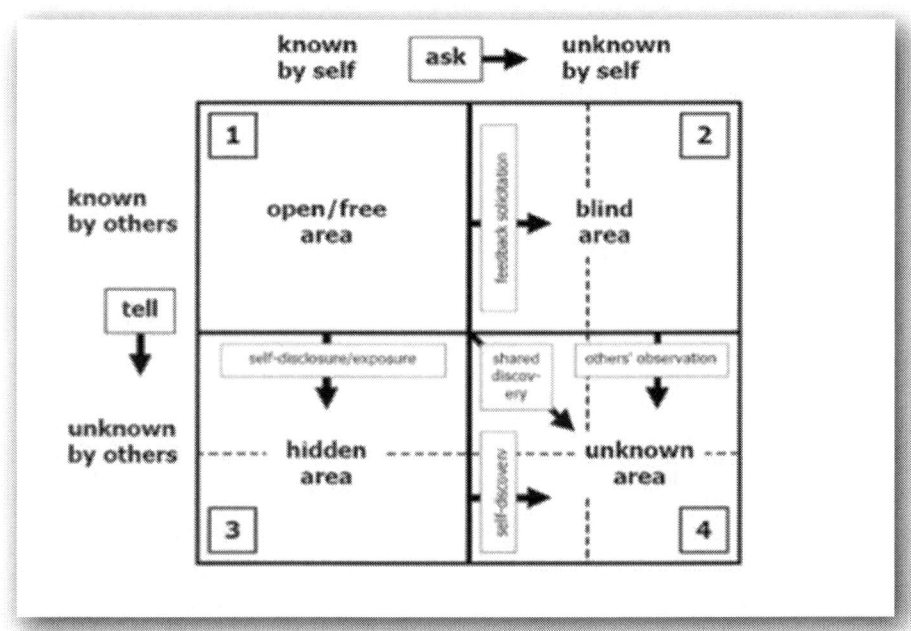

Fig. 24 Johari window

Johari's model consists of a window with four panes.

The most effective area for a leader to work in is the open pane. Here we have transparency, clarity and mutual understanding, many of the characteristics of high levels of trust. The hidden pane contains those things the leader know about themselves, but the followers do not know about them. This will gradually open as trust develops between the leader and the followers and the leader reveals more about themselves. This will lead to an increase in the size of the open pane. The unknown pane is the area containing things the leader and the followers do not know, for example, things that have not been tried or problems not yet faced so that capabilities are not yet known. As the organisation and the relationship between leader and followers mature and the leader tries new things and faces new experiences this pane opens up. The dangerous pane in terms of leadership is the blind pane. This contains things the followers know about the leader but the leaders not aware of themselves. An example of this would be the effect the leader has on other people within the organisation. The only way to open up this pane is to get feedback. In education we are often very sensitive about feedback. This could be because as we have seen SELF (see figure 18) plays such a large role in what we do. However, if we reflect on the fact that most often feedback is the gap between intention and perception, it is always useful to have. One common way of investigating the gap between intention and perception is 360 degree feedback. This is especially useful if the feedback is gathered anonymously as it will be more accurate. Feedback gathered in this way can be used by the recipient to check what others say about them against their own beliefs and intentions. In my experience this is best done outside of performance management and rather as an aid for reflection on personal effectiveness.

USING APPRECIATIVE INQUIRY TO GET FEEDBACK

Another useful approach when getting feedback in sensitive areas is to use appreciative enquiry methodology. As we have seen previously, this can be used as an approach to planning change but it can also be used as an approach to getting feedback. This technique gathers feedback by using questions that can only generate positive answers. This may sound a rather anodyne process but in fact is sometimes a very useful way of getting truthful feedback since there is no incentive in not being honest. The questions also often prompt people to tell stories 'do you remember the time that......'. Stories are often far richer in information compared with questionnaires. Below are some questions I have used to help Headteachers get feedback using the appreciative inquiry methodology.

> When am I most positive?
> When am I most enthusiastic?
> What behaviours do I role model?
> What is my best quality as a leader?
> What values do I articulate?
> What is my best quality as a team member?
> What is the most important thing I do in the school?
> What do I do to build good relationships with and between staff?
> When am I most helpful in supporting you in doing your job?
> What is the most effective thing I do to support you when you have difficulties?
> When you want support what behaviours do I exhibit that are most supportive?
> What has been the best change I have introduced?

A Headteacher I worked with used this list to gather the views of staff and was surprised to find that a majority felt the most important thing he did in the school was lead assemblies. This was not the answer he was expecting and so was very useful feedback. They felt that in assemblies they got a real feel for what he believed, what was important and how things were going. After this he considered very carefully how he could make assemblies even more useful! I am sure that he would have preferred staff to have identified some other aspect of his work but the feedback also helped him to understand that if this was to be the perception in the future he would have to give this preferred outcome a higher priority. The same method can be used to get feedback about Governors and from parents. For example:

> What does your child enjoy most in school?
> What is the best bit about the school newsletter?
> What do you think I stand for as a Headteacher?
> What do I care about as a Headteacher?
> What values does the school give a high priority to?
> What is the best thing the school does to encourage good behaviour?
> What is the most important thing the Governing Body does?
> When do you think the Governing Body are most effective in communicating with parents?
> When are the Governors most supportive of the school?
> What is the most important responsibility that Governors take on?
> When are Governors most supportive of staff?
> When are Governors most supportive of parents?

This is also a particularly useful technique for staff to use to get feedback from children about their learning in a way that avoids judging the teacher but nonetheless generates really useful information in terms of improving learning. Examples of questions that could be used are:

> What makes learning fun?
> What is the most important thing you have learnt about learning?
> What is the best thing about this school?
> Who is the best person to speak to if you have a problem?
> What is the best thing a teacher can do to help your learning?

Since Daniel Goleman (1998) developed the concept of Emotional Intelligence, EI has increasingly been seen as a key indicator of effective potential leaders. Goleman's work indicates that leaders who are self-aware will be able to manage their skills and emotions more effectively as well as having greater empathy with others. Thus they are likely to have a positive impact on the people they work with.

Getting feedback and acting as a coach are two ways in which I believe a leader can build their EI hence the importance of finding ways of getting honest feedback.

Building Resilience.

Resilience is often described as a personal quality that predisposes individuals to bounce back after setbacks. In education this is an essential quality to try to develop as a Headteacher. The role has always been demanding but with the very high levels of accountability that now exist, together with the increasing number of difficult situations Headteachers now have to deal with, high levels of resilience have become essential.

Headteachers also need to monitor signals of flagging resilience within their schools. Indicators include:

> Top leaders fail to keep learning.
> People blame everything on the budget or some other problem outside their control.
> Leaders ignore critical indicators.
> Too many initiatives drain people.
> Success goes uncelebrated.

As individuals there are strategies that have proved useful in building resilience. These include:

> Don't forget to do things you enjoy.
> Stay optimistic.

Choose your words carefully to create a positive climate.
Don't become defensive when something goes wrong.
Cultivate networks.
Use other people's insights and strengths.

Being Creative

Headteachers regularly grapple with many complex and difficult issues. Being creative in these situations can add a great deal to your effectiveness. Many people, however, believe that creativity cannot be taught and that some leaders are just born more creative than others. In reality this is only partially true and we can develop creativity. The following are characteristics of creative leadership which can be developed:

- A focus on solutions and opportunities rather than problems but good at solving problems
- Intellectual curiosity
- Simplicity over complexity
- Recognising other's strengths and gifts
- Reflection is a key leadership behaviour and priority

The role of a creative leader is also not to have all the ideas; it's to create a culture where everyone can have ideas and feel that they are valued. So it's much more about creating climates where others can be involved and valued as part of a solution- focussed organisation.

The toolkit for creativity includes

- Using research
- Brainstorming
- SWOT analysis
- Rapid piloting
- Mind mapping

All of these tools empower others to contribute and to release the creativity within an organisation.

Key points
Reflect regularly on how you can improve your skills as a leader.
Don't duck difficult conversations – your team won't forgive you.
Extend and build trust.

Further reading:
Covey S, (1989). *The Seven Habits of Highly Effective People*. Free Press ISBN 0-671-70863-5.
Goleman D, Boyatis R, McKee A, (2002) *The New Leaders*. Time Warner.

CHAPTER 7

Motivation

• • •

'Really great people make you feel that you, too, can be great'

Mark Twain

If you ask teachers to describe their Headteacher they almost always describe the things their Headteacher does rather than any deeply held beliefs or values. If you ask them to describe Headteachers who are generally recognised as exceptional the two things they say most often are that the Headteacher motivates staff and tackles the difficult issues. Being able to motivate staff is crucial to building a successful school but achieving this is not always easy. In terms of the role of the Headteacher in helping to motivate staff, it is generally agreed that they must be positive and model hopefulness and enthusiasm. This is especially important at times of stress for the school but is easier said than done on wet morning in January! However, it is essential that the Head does stay hopeful because otherwise we give staff carte blanche to be negative. Although Heads usually recognise the importance of motivation and the part it plays in achieving success, very few have a developed a comprehensive strategy for motivating staff. Some are keen to recognise and praise the work of staff or show that they are valued by providing good quality venues for Inset etc. These are useful things to do but do not allow for the fact that individual staff are motivated in very different ways.

MOTIVATION AND THE WORK OF HERTZBERG.

One of the most useful pieces of research on motivation was carried out by Hertzberg (1959). He investigated the motivational effect of a number of variables. His results are summarised below. They show that satisfaction and dissatisfaction arise from different factors and are not simply opposing reactions to the same factors. We can see that some factors truly motivate while others, which he called hygiene factors, lead to dissatisfaction. Thus in organisations it is not enough to eliminate hygiene factors, we also need to put in place opportunities for staff to gain satisfaction.

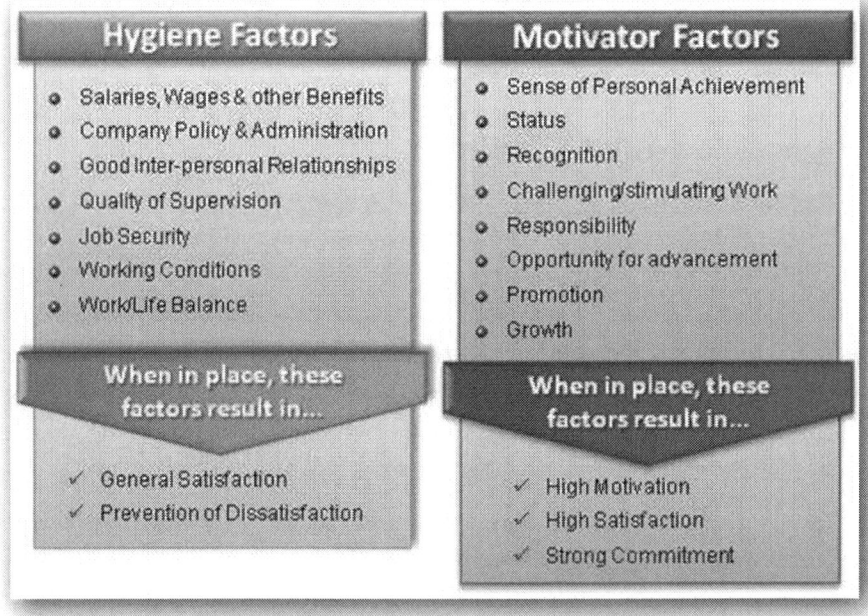

Hygiene Factors
- Salaries, Wages & other Benefits
- Company Policy & Administration
- Good Inter-personal Relationships
- Quality of Supervision
- Job Security
- Working Conditions
- Work/Life Balance

When in place, these factors result in...
- General Satisfaction
- Prevention of Dissatisfaction

Motivator Factors
- Sense of Personal Achievement
- Status
- Recognition
- Challenging/stimulating Work
- Responsibility
- Opportunity for advancement
- Promotion
- Growth

When in place, these factors result in...
- High Motivation
- High Satisfaction
- Strong Commitment

Fig. 25 Hertzberg motivators and hygiene factors

The lesson from the Hertzberg research is that nothing motivates everybody. Motivation therefore needs to be personalised and we need to find out what motivates our staff on an individual basis and how we can respond to this. Line Management/Performance Management meetings provide a good opportunity to have a discussion about motivation.

Research about what teachers value is also interesting; the list of results is shown below:

- Participation in decision making,
- Use of valued skills
- Freedom and independence
- Challenge
- Expression of creativity
- Opportunity for learning

Many of the things that teachers value would flow from the sort of accountability structure already discussed and an effective Professional Learning Community would also go a long way to providing opportunities for staff to do things they value.

Keeping yourself motivated.

As a Headteacher the most important person of all to keep motivated is you because if you as the Head become de-motivated it has a hugely negative effect on the school. Headteachers often neglect their own motivation though, preferring to concentrate on others. I have worked with many Headteachers, usually some years into post, who, when asked what they did last week that they enjoyed, struggle to come up with an answer. As a leader it is always useful to remind yourself why you wanted the job and to continue doing at least some of these things you enjoy. I believe it is also a mistake to begin to think that you can't go out on a course or visit other schools because of feelings of guilt at being away from the school. If you are lucky your Governing Body will see it as their responsibility to ensure that you are motivated and again your Performance Management meeting is a good time to address this.

Really effective staff development is also often motivational for staff and giving this a correspondingly high importance in the work of the school will demonstrate that you value staff.

Motivating non-teaching support staff is often a problem in schools because they are in general very poorly paid and we know from Hertzberg's work that this can be very de-motivating. A lot of schools have tried to show they value the work of these staff by including them in Inset days and some schools have progress meetings which involve both the teacher and the teaching assistant linked to the class. This has the added bonus of increasing accountability as well as showing that the work of teaching assistants is valued. The most effective strategies will take into account that staff react differently to change. A simple example of this emerged in an evaluation into the effectiveness of Continual Professional Development (CPD) I carried out at a large comprehensive school. Office staff said they appreciated that the SLT were keen to include them in all the activities on Inset days but that spending time listening to topics which had no direct bearing on their daily work was of limited use. They would have preferred visiting other schools to see how roles were carried out in a different context. I think this just shows the importance of not assuming groups of staff of staff can be motivated in the same way; a more sophisticated personalised strategy is required.

Occasionally as a leader you come across a person who is very hard to motivate. A useful approach is to use the technique we discussed earlier of giving them ownership of the issue by stating the behaviour and then using silence to make them respond and take ownership of it. 'You seem very difficult to motivate. What would motivate you to do better in your role?' These techniques are useful because the only person who can do anything about these problems is the person with the problem and the first step towards this is for them to own the problem. Finally, I do not know where this quote comes from but it resonates for me and I believe does capture some wisdom about how you can motivate your staff:

'One of the Headteacher's most important roles is to remind teachers every day of the vital role they play in the lives of their students and of the high expectations their communities hold for them'

KEY POINTS
Do something you enjoy every day.
Spend time regularly motivating staff.
Remember not everybody is motivated in the same way as you!

FURTHER READING:
McClelland D, (1988). *Human Motivation.* Cambridge University Press ISBN10-0521369517
Pintrich P, Schunk D, (1995). *Motivation in* Education: *Theory Research and Application.* Pearson

CHAPTER 8
Managing the Organisation

• • •

'Management is doing things right, leadership is doing the right things'

PETER DRUCKER

ALTHOUGH LESS EXCITING FOR MOST leaders, good management plays an important role in achieving success and, more importantly, maintaining success in a school. The amount of help you have to support you in the management of the school can vary enormously. I have worked with Headteachers of very small schools who had only part-time secretaries and often ended up answering the phone. Although no Headteacher would want to do this I think the reality of small schools is that inevitably Heads do end up doing things we would not expect them to do. In these situations the unfortunate reality is often about trying to reduce the number of occasions this happens in order to manage more effectively.

USING THE SUPPORT AVAILABLE.
Fortunately most Headteachers do have significant support to help them manage the school and the issue then is how to make the most of that support. Your personal assistant or secretary should play a key role in helping you avoid spending unnecessary time on management tasks others should be doing. Often, in order to help them achieve this, you may have to invest

some up-front time so they learn how to carry out the role in the way you want. I worked recently with a Headteacher who complained about the time he spent answering emails and opening mail. He didn't feel he could leave this to his secretary as there had been problems in the past with letters going to the wrong staff etc. The strategy we used to solve this was that for a week he did these tasks with his secretary beside him and explained how and why he dealt with each email or letter in particular way. The next week the secretary did all of the letters and emails but forwarded to the Head all the emails and letters where she wasn't sure who should deal with them. Already he was saving time but he now further explained how and why he was going to deal with those she forwarded to him. He did this every time until she very rarely bothered him again but dealt with the task as well as he would have.

This type of approach, being absolutely explicit about the type and detail of the support you need, although initially time consuming, always pays dividends. Another example might be using the same approach to establish which calls are to be put through to you and which to other staff or when the bursar/administrative assistant has to check expenditure with you etc. This explicitness is also needed in important areas such as how support staff should talk to learners, how they answer telephones and greet parents and visitors. This is a much more successful approach than hoping that they pick these things up by some sort of osmosis process! Where you inherit support staff who are not working in the way you would like, for example, not being very welcoming to parents, one way to change this is actually to have a dialogue about how this should be done. In my experience, even staff working in a dysfunctional way can usually describe how the job should be done. Your task then is to remind them of what they said should be the way of working whenever they fall below this agreed standard. In time the new behaviour will embed. Another important way to ensure that you get the most from your support staff is to make certain you put in place effective performance management arrangements for them. In many schools this is does not happen and can result in support staff being de-motivated and feeling less valued as well as being less effective.

Increasingly Academy Trusts are taking on the role of providing financial and Human Resources advice and support. This centralised assistance can be very helpful for small schools where the level of support available to the Headteacher can be minimal.

THE IMPORTANCE OF GOOD COMMUNICATION.

One essential aspect of good management is good communication. When communication is poor it is a recipe for frustration for both staff and leaders. Headteachers use a range of ways of communicating with staff including daily or weekly briefings, email or weekly bulletins, meetings, assemblies and often a combination of all of these. Where possible, limiting the amount of time spent communicating information at team meetings will mean more time can be spent on the really important issues related to teaching and learning issues. Whatever strategies you adopt in terms of communication it is important to review the effectiveness with staff on a regular basis to ensure it is fit for purpose. You will personally need to be a good and confident communicator and if this does not come naturally it should become an area of focus for developing your personal effectiveness.

Many Headteachers complain that they have less control over their agenda than a class teacher because they never know what problem will walk through the door or who will phone, for example. We have already touched on how to manage who should have access to the Headteacher. Just because someone asks for the Headteacher does not mean that the Head is the right person to deal with the issue they have. This is often true of the more official requests Heads get from people who want to come to meet them. Examples might be staff from property services, contractors etc. Many hours can be tied up over a year in meetings that really would have been just as effective if the Deputy or some other member of staff had been present rather than the Head. Questioning why the meeting has to be with the Head can sometimes avoid this. After all what would happen if you were ill? Some Headteachers pride themselves on having an open door policy but the reality is this can make it too easy to see the Headteacher and too easy to distract them from what they should be doing.

Monitoring

Management is about maintenance rather than change and an important part of maintenance is monitoring and checking. There are many successful changes which, when moved into maintenance, wither and die because monitoring and checking was not done properly and the school is then faced with another unnecessary change process to get back to where it was previously. Many people feel an aversion to be checked up on as is evidenced by the Hertzberg (1959) research where supervision can be a big de-motivator. This can be overcome to a degree by being very clear about the checking procedures you are going to use, and when and why you are checking up. The purpose of this is to try to gain acceptance. However, unless leaders tackle the difficult issues that sometimes arise from monitoring none of this will be effective. Staff who have not been following procedures, for example, need to be faced with this and the fact that they are letting the school down. They are the only people who can put this right but they must be made to take ownership of the issue.

All Headteachers are involved in monitoring teaching which is the probably the most important aspect of the monitoring work they do. Work sampling, however, can also be a very useful and informative monitoring technique. Where monitoring is carried out by other members of the leadership team it is very important to ensure consistency in terms of judgement. This is essential not just in terms of achieving a rigorous approach but also in terms of fairness to staff. A system of joint observation and work sampling can help to achieve this consistency and is good development. It will also be necessary to benchmark the school's judgements against standards in other schools. This may be done by working with a consultant who has experience of this or through working with colleagues in other schools. Giving timely feedback after monitoring activities is very important. There are many techniques for doing this; getting staff to reflect themselves on how well something has been done, giving a number of good points and a development point etc. Usually these are very useful but I think if you have observed something you believe to be unsatisfactory it is very important that you are clear about this at the beginning of the feedback so that there can be no misunderstanding.

Budgets.

Monitoring budgets, ensuring financial probity and sound financial planning are also key roles for the Headteacher. There will often be support systems in place to support you in these areas but ultimately it is the Headteacher who carries the responsibility for ensuring all of these are in place.

In order to do this you will need to be familiar with the different funding streams for the school and how they are predicted to change, historic, present and future expenditure plans, and how the School Improvement Plan and Strategic Plan is related to the current budget and future budgets.

The monitoring of current expenditure against budget is also important but there are usually robust systems to facilitate this. Falling budgets are always a difficult issue to manage. Dealing with this often involves looking for efficiencies and ways for increasing income. However, given that so much of the school budget is spent on staff salaries, this will often be the focus of cuts. This can sometimes lead the Headteacher into taking difficult decisions involving people losing their jobs. If this happens the driving force for all decisions must be what is in the best interests of the children tempting though it may be to tread paths which appear easier to follow.

Key points

Be explicit about the support you need.
Remember communication is a two way process-check others think it is good.
Check to ensure that important tasks are carried out

Further reading:
Blanchard K, Johnson S, (1982). *One minute manager* Publisher William Morrow & Co.
ISBN 9780006367536
Davies B & West-Burnham J, (2003) *The Handbook of Educational Leadership and Management.* Pearson

CHAPTER 9

Working with Governors

• • •

'None of us is as smart as all of us'

Ken Blanchard

During my career in education I have spent fourteen years as a Headteacher and twenty five years as a Governor so I have seen the importance of the relationship between Heads and Governors from both sides. I have also chaired two Interim Executive Boards (IEB), which gives a very interesting new insight into effective Governance. (An Interim Executive Board can be set up by a Local Authority or the Department for Education after removing a Governing Body. This sometimes occurs when a school is in difficulty.) The conclusion I have drawn from these experiences is that Governors have a very difficult job to do in order to carry out their responsibilities, given the time they usually have to do so.

The three statutory roles that Governors are given are to set the strategic direction of the school, act as a critical friend and hold the school to account. In addition, Governors are responsible for the performance management of the Headteacher. Monitoring the budget and ensuring financial probity are also key responsibilities. The reality is that they will have very little time to carry out these roles; full governing bodies often meet only 5 or 6 times a year. In my experience the most effective Governing Bodies are those that find a way to make the work involved in carrying out their role more manageable. You can play an important role in helping them to do this. The Beckhard model for effective teams, that we considered earlier (figure 21), can also be applied to Governing Bodies. I have seen many Governors who, because they never understood what the goals were, were then unable to see what their role involved and did not engage effectively in the work of the Governing Body. These Governors sometimes say very little in meetings or else tend to go off at tangents because they have no clear idea of what they should be doing.

Thus the first task in developing an effective Governing Body is to develop with them a vivid vision or strategic direction for the school. However, the strategic direction of the school must be underpinned by the core beliefs and values. In my work with Governing Bodies one of the things I have often discovered is that they have never actually sat down with the Headteacher and discussed what are their core, shared beliefs about learning. They will typically have spent a lot of time talking about relationships and the way they want people to work together but there is no agreement about learning, the core purpose of the school. If a Governing Body has not had this type of discussion, setting a strategic direction and importantly making sure you are not blown off course, is much more difficult. Having a framework of beliefs against which proposed changes and initiatives can be tested is also important to the authenticity of the Governing Body. The most effective Governing Bodies work with the Head and SLT and, through them, the staff, to develop a strategic direction or plan which will often involve changes in the culture of the school, e.g. developing the skill levels of staff that require them to learn new behaviours or changes in curriculum priorities or content. These types of developments can rarely be achieved quickly and must be worked on over a longer timescale.

The 'critical friend' aspect of the role of Governors has caused much controversy and has been problematic for some relationships between Governors and Headteachers. One of the interesting experiences when chairing an Interim Executive Board is that after a year, the IEB has to set up and work with a Shadow Governing Body which develops into a normal Governing Body over time. Setting up a Shadow Governing Body forces a focus on how the key roles of the Governing Body will be carried out.

Good questions for Governors

When considering what a critical friend would look like, for example, it was felt in the IEBs I chaired, that this involved asking challenging questions in order to add value to the SLT's thinking. Thus a number of questions were developed which are shown below. Governors find these extremely useful but soon get the hang of asking their own good questions in order to challenge thinking but in a supportive way. The questions we used are shown below:

> What alternatives did you consider?
> Why was this method chosen?
> Do all schools do it this way?
> Why do other schools choose a different method?
> Have we any evidence to support this choice?
> What are the downsides of this decision?
> What will we gain by doing this?
> Are the gains we are going to get worth the effort in terms of staff time?
> If we do this how will we know it has been successful?
> What are the implications for your time if we do this?
> How does this fit in with our strategic objectives?
> How will this impact on learning?

Governors found this type of approach helpful in terms of the critical friend role and quickly learned to ask their own questions. This emphasises the importance of the training in helping Governors to be effective. One way of ensuring this becomes a priority is to have a Governor with responsibility for auditing and meeting training needs as well as organising a regular review of the work of the Governing body.

Holding the school to account is probably the easiest of the three roles of the Governing Body in that they are supported in this work by Ofsted inspections and the results from national tests. However, as we have seen before, accountability means different things to different people and deciding on the way accountability will be exercised by the Governing Body is an important decision to make.

In my experience it is far healthier to define accountability in terms of answerability than associating it with an over focus on blame.

I would now like to consider other areas of the work of Governing Bodies.

Establishing key performance indicators

Often one of the main focuses of Governors meetings is progress against the School Improvement plan. Often this plan is quite a long document and the reality is that there probably isn't time to monitor this effectively and, in trying to do so, what happens is that Governors have very little understanding of most of the plan. The other problem with the typical School Improvement Plan is that all the tasks appear equally important whereas in reality some will be much more important than others. This is the key to making the process manageable in the time available for the Governing Body meetings. If you work with the Governors to identify perhaps two or three of the key issues, the ones that will be most important to raising standards, then these Key Performance Indicators can become a focus of discussion on a regular basis at meetings. This means that over a period Governors can achieve a good understanding of these key issues. You can, of course, report progress with regard to the other elements of the plan but there would not be an assumption that these would be discussed unless there was a reason.

Many Governing Bodies have adopted a system of sub-committees in order to manage the work load. This can be an efficient use of time as long as the purpose and authority of the committee is clearly defined so that the work is not repeated in the full Governing Body meeting as can sometimes be the case. There are an increasing number of Governing Bodies, often the ones with fewer members, who use individual governors to take on specific roles rather than sub-committees. These governing bodies will often meet more frequently than is usually the case, but of course, do not have to attend other sub-committee meetings. This can also be a very efficient system.

The advent of 'Trust status,' 'hard and soft federations', Academies and Free Schools has meant that the models of Governance have become more diverse. However, I believe all the points made are equally valid for any of the new models.

Relationship between the Head and Chair of Governors

One of the key relationships within a school is that between the Headteacher and the Chair of Governors. Where this is effective the relationship will be friendly but not cosy, supportive but challenging. Recently the NCTL has developed a course for Chairs and Aspiring Chairs which is designed to help Chairs develop this sort of approach.

It is essential nowadays that an element of challenge exists but this can be done effectively by asking the right question rather direct criticism. The analysis below characterises the sorts of relationship that can exist between Heads and Governors but the only safe one for a Headteacher, especially in view of Ofsted judgement but also for good governance, is the Partners or critical friends section.

```
                      High Support

   Supporters Club          Partners or critical
                                  friends
   "We're here to
   support the head!"       "We're here to share
                            everything - good or
                                   bad."

Low Challenge                      High Challenge


      Abdicators                Adversaries

   "We leave it to           "We keep a very
   the professionals:        close eye on the head."
        staff!"

                       Low Support
```

Fig. 26 Support challenge analysis

The role of the Chair of Governors in organising the work of the governors, drawing up agendas and ensuring governors are well informed, is essential for good governance. Efficient chairing of meetings and ensuring that time is spent on the important issues is also crucial. Inevitably in order to carry out the role effectively the Chair will need to meet regularly with you. However, it is important to establish what the purpose of these meetings is so that an appropriate frequency can be decided upon. Sometimes, if these meetings take place too regularly, there is a temptation to talk too much about day-to-day issues which is not the role of governance.

When the relationship between the Governors is ineffective the Headteacher often finds himself/herself spending a lot of time servicing the governing body but the work does not add much value to the leadership of the school. Where there is an effective relationship Governors help shape the thinking of the SLT by providing a wider perspective on the issues facing the school, are effective in helping other stakeholders in the community understand the work of the school and challenge areas of underperformance in order to raise standards. A rule of thumb, for identifying how effective your Governors are, is to think about who does all the talking at Governors meetings. If it is always you the meetings are probably not effective!

Key points
Helping your Governors to be effective helps you.
Make the work of Governors manageable.
Develop an effective professional relationship with the Chair

Read on:
Gann N, (1997). *Improving School Governance.* Routledge 1997 ISBN 0750706759
Sallis J,(2000). *Heads in Partnership: Working with Your Governors for a Successful School.* Pearson
Ofsted, (2011) *School Governance Learning from the best.* Available from the Ofsted website

CHAPTER 10

Working with other stakeholders

• • •

'You never know the power of the network of another person'

BOB KEITH

DURING RECENT YEARS SCHOOLS HAVE begun to engage with a wider range of stakeholders partly in response to political initiatives - Every Child Matters, The Children's Plan and Social Cohesion initiatives would be some of the most important of these. However, schools have always tried to work within the community and not in isolation from it. The most important stakeholders they seek to engage with are, of course, parents. We know from the work of Charles Desforges (2003) that parents have a much greater influence than schools throughout Primary education and well into Secondary school. This research has spurred schools on to try to engage more effectively with parents in terms of their children's learning because of the potential improvement in standards that could be achieved if the efforts of parents and school can be aligned.

WORKING IN PARTNERSHIP WITH PARENTS.
For many years schools have talked about working in partnership with parents but to what extent this actually happens varies enormously. If you

listen in to the sort of conversation that typically takes place at a parents' consultation evening you rarely hear the language of partnership, it is much more usually characterised by the implicit message 'I am the professional and I am telling you…' Of course it is true that the teacher is the professional but it is not the language of partnership and does not acknowledge the huge role parents play in children's learning. We often pay lip service to the fact that a lot of learning takes place outside of school but have not yet begun to see how we can fully utilise this learning in schools.

Some schools I have worked with have tackled this issue by trying to establish a common understanding with parents of what learning is and 'what it looks like in this school'. I am not talking about curriculum information evenings about the topics children are covering, useful though this might be, but a chance to actually try out learning in the same way children do in the same classrooms. This approach, although more difficult to organise because it often involves having parents in school during the day, is far more effective in forging a partnership with parents because it begins to build a consensus about what learning is. Schools are also engaging with parents in terms of parenting classes. These have also proved very useful although they have to be delivered in a way that avoids building a deficit model which would reinforce the 'I'm a professional and know what's best for you' message which might prove counter-cultural to the partnership you want to build.

In New Zealand they have developed some excellent resources for use by parents who want to support their child's learning. Many aspects of these can be used with parents in this country.

Link: http://nzcurriculum.tki.org.nz/National-Standards/Supporting-parents-and-whanau/Resources

Feedback-again!

Another important aspect of working with parents is set to up regular opportunities for them to give honest feedback on how the school is doing. We are much more familiar with this because of our experience of Ofsted inspections and the kind of surveys used as part of the inspection process. However, some schools are much more proactive in seeking feedback than others and this is another area where you can take a lead and model openness to feedback. As Bill Gates is quoted as saying 'your most unhappy customer is your best source of feedback for improvement'. If a school begins to lose the confidence of parents Heads need to be aware of this very quickly and intervene to re-build confidence. Regular feedback can act as an early warning system as well as giving positive messages about what parents value. In his book 'Schools must speak for themselves' John MacBeath (1999) suggests developing a core set of questions that could be used across a range of stakeholders. There are many advantages to this approach. Using a shared language for gathering views of children, parents, governors, teachers and support staff ensures greater consistency in how you are able to interpret answers to the questions. Using core questions that can be used over a number of years also means that trends can be reliably established which will make the data generated much more usable. Carrying out such surveys in a way that parents can choose to engage anonymously, will also make it more likely the feedback is honest. Demonstrating to parents that you have acted on at least some of the feedback is a good way to build a partnership. Most schools have a Parent Teacher Association which can often act as a springboard for some of these developments

MAKING SCHOOL ACCESSIBLE TO PARENTS.

For many parents schools are still rather intimidating places to visit. Schools are generally very good at making public areas welcoming in trying to overcome some of this anxiety although as someone who regularly telephones schools I personally find automated reply systems, especially those that eventually cut you off, a little unwelcoming. A more positive development, however, has been the development of the role of Parental Support Officer. This person will often act as a bridge between school and the parent, an advocate for the school with the parent and an advocate for the parent with the school. They will typically not be a teacher but will have good people skills and be able to work with parents effectively. Large secondary schools regularly have staff appointed to this type of role but for small primary schools they only way to access such expertise would be through a cluster arrangement.

Working in Networks

For many years it has been recognised that there is a big potential gain to be made by using community links to make the curriculum more relevant for children. The reality is that often these links are very time consuming to establish and then maintain. I have worked with a few clusters of schools which have realised that this is an area where they can work effectively together for their mutual advantage and the mutual advantage of their learners. This can be done in a variety of ways, everything from simply building a common data base of contacts to allocating responsibility for maintaining certain contacts to certain schools. This type of cluster working is another way of working with other stakeholders. For Primary schools clusters and 'hard and soft federations' provide opportunities for everything from improved professional learning, to access to the expertise of Business Managers, ICT managers and Human Resources staff that would be beyond the budget of individual schools. At a time when more and more schools are becoming Academies and taking on tasks that were previously carried out by Local Authorities having access to this type of expertise is becoming almost essential.

Combining Inset days and other CPD activities can also reduce the cost for each school and enable them to work with people with national as well as local reputations that they would probably be unable to afford individually. Mutual coaching between staff in different schools is also an option that some teachers prefer because they can work with colleagues with whom they don't have quite such a close relationship. I have worked with a number of schools that have set up coaching partnerships for Middle Leaders in different schools e.g. between Literacy co-ordinators, or Heads of Mathematics Departments. Networks like these also offer the opportunity for improving Best Value options by combining the buying power of schools. One useful step when trying to build these types of relationships with other schools is to ensure that at the same time as relationships are being built between the staff at the schools they are also developed between the Governors. This can be done by arranging regular meetings of the Chairs and Headteachers and will help overcome the parochial perspective that sometimes understandably occurs in governing bodies of smaller schools.

In terms of schools working together in networks, we work in exciting times! The new political agenda has set out a reduced role for Local Authorities and the prospect of schools taking on more responsibilities for themselves. This change has been coming over a long period but has certainly accelerated with the prospect of most schools adopting Academy status in the coming years and as Local Authorities find it increasingly difficult to provide the wide ranging support that was available in the past. Many schools have seized this opportunity to begin to work together in areas of mutual interest in order to be more effective. Groups of schools working together have the capacity to take on many of the things traditionally done by Local Authorities but to make the support more personalised to their needs and therefore more effective.

Most Headteachers inherit a series of networks on appointment many of which may have existed for a long time and there is some pressure just to continue to go to these meetings. I think this temptation needs to be examined in the light of the new paradigm that schools are working in. There are real gains to be made from effective networks of schools that are open to sharing and working together but if this isn't the case then staying in networks that are not useful is time consuming and wasteful of effort. The experience of the Network Learning Communities set up by David Jackson at NCSL was that networks function much better if they are facilitated and the group actually designate a member to take on this role. This can be done on a rotational basis but is one way to ensure the network functions effectively. Even so, networks often have a limited time span in terms of usefulness and you need to regularly ask yourself the question 'are these meetings useful in terms of helping me raise standards?'

Since the proposal to make it optional to work with a School Improvement Partner came into force there is also great potential for Headteachers to use their networks, not just for problem solving and ideas generation, but also to benchmark their own judgements about standards. This might be done with a National Leader of Education, a Local Leader of Education or a colleague Head with whom you are already working and whose judgement you value. Peer review of this type has a lot of potential as long as the protocols are clear and the approach is honest and rigorous. Such arrangements are not only valuable in terms of evaluation but are excellent professional learning opportunities. This type of networking can, of course, also be international nowadays. Visiting schools in other countries is often a powerful learning experience for Headteachers and even where resources make this difficult the use of Skype can help link staff in schools in different countries who may be addressing similar issues and able to help each other.

Although the value of networks is almost universally acknowledged in education the reality can be that we work in an environment in which competition between schools exists and if anything is growing, often promoted by the political agenda. David Hargreaves, in his work on 'Creating a self-improving school system' talks of competition not being the opposite of co-operation, in other words competition between schools should not rule out co-operation where they have mutual interests. In deciding which networks to work with or to form you will need to be confident that you are working with colleagues who all feel there is a mutual advantage to gain and thus a reason to share what they know.

SOMETIMES IT'S THE SMALL THINGS THAT COUNT MOST!

In concluding what I hope you have found to be a useful, practical guide to successful Headship, I would just like to share one other observation I have made about successful leaders. Sometimes it is not the big things you do that have the biggest impact. Malcolm Gladwell (2000) makes the same point in his book 'The Tipping Point'. I can think of examples of this from my own Headship. When I started as a Head I decided that at each assembly I would read out the names of three pupils and ask them to bring all their books the next day so that we could discuss their work. This had a far greater effect on standards than I could ever imagine. Of course it was not a panacea but it did tighten marking and assessment and increased motivation for a lot of pupils. I have seen similar things happen in other schools when working with Headteachers. One Head changed all the signs within the school which read 'Children' to 'Learners'. When you walked around that school this really made an impression and was an effective statement about their priorities and beliefs.

NEXT STEPS.

Unbelievably the job that once seemed so impossible eventually becomes much easier to cope with. Indeed many Heads find themselves looking for challenges and things to do outside of their own school. This is an understandable and healthy situation for some Heads but there will be others for whom the job in their school will always be what they need to fulfil their ambitions. Fortunately, nowadays there are many opportunities for Headteachers who have a desire to work in other schools. As well as the opportunity to move to a new Headship other options are now available. Executive Headship of more than one school, working within a Federation of schools, working as a Local Leader of Education or a National Leader of Education all offer this type of opportunity.

Wherever you career takes you it in important never to forget that Headship is a privilege because it provides a chance to prepare the next generation to make their mark on the world and pass on the culture of previous generations. I would urge you to treat it as a privilege, remember to smile and enjoy it, and look for the tipping points!

Key points

Look at the school from the parents' perspective and evidence the judgements you make.
Work with other schools to make your school more efficient and effective
Ensure you have access to quality support where needed

Further reading:

Harris A, Andrew-Power K, Goodall J (2009). *Do Parents Know They Matter? Raising Achievement Through Parental Engagement.* Network Continuum

Jackson D, (2002). *The creation of knowledge networks. Collaborative Enquiry for School and System Improvement.* (Paper presented to the CERI/OECD/DfES/QCA/ESRC Forum "Knowledge Management in Education and Learning", Oxford.)

REFERENCES

• • •

Anderson, L. W., Krathwohl, D. R., Airasian, P. W., Cruikshank, K. A., Mayer, R. E., Pintrich, P. R., Raths, J., Wittrock, M. C. (2000). *A Taxonomy for Learning, Teaching, and Assessing: A revision of Bloom's Taxonomy of Educational Objectives*. New York: Pearson, Allyn & Bacon.

Beckhard, R, (1969). *Organization Development: Strategies and Models*, Addison-Wesley, Reading

Beckhard R, (1972). *Optimising Team Building Efforts*, Journal of Contemporary Business

Belbin M, (1981). *Management Teams*, London; Heinemann. ISBN 0470271728.

Biggs J., Collis, K. (1982) *Evaluating the Quality of Learning: the SOLO taxonomy*. New York: Academic Press

Bloom B (1956). *Taxonomy of Educational Objectives, Handbook I: The Cognitive Domain*. New York: David McKay Co Inc.

Bloom, B. (1968). *Learning for Mastery*. Instruction and Curriculum. Regional Education Laboratory for the Carolinas and Virginia, Topical Papers and Reprints.

Boyatzis, R E, (1999) *Self-directed change and learning as a necessary meta-competency for success and effectiveness in the 21st century.* In Sims, R. and Veres, J.G. (eds.). Keys to employee success in the coming decades. Westport, CN: Greenwood Publishing

Burns J M, (1978). *Leadership.* NY Harper and Row.

Collins J, (2001). *Good to Great.* Harper Business ISBN:9780066620992

Cooperrider D, Srivastva S, (1987) *Research in Organisational Change and Development.* Volume 1 pp 129-169, JAI press

Covey S. R. (1989). *The Seven Habits of Highly Effective People.* Free Press. ISBN 0-671-70863-5.

Covey, S. R., (1990). *Principle-centered leadership.* New York : Fireside

Covey S(Junior), Merrill R, (2006.) *The Speed of Trust* : The One Thing that Changes Everything, Simon & Schuster Adult Publishing Group ISBN-13: 9780743297301

Desforges C, Aboucaar A. (2003) *The impact of parental involvement, parental support and family education on pupil achievement adjustment: a review of the literature* DFE publication Queen's Printer. ISBN 1 84185 999 0

Drucker P, (2002). *On Leading Change*: A leader to leader guide Rob Johnston *(Editor)*, Frances Hesselbein*(Editor)*   Wiley, John & Sons, Incorporated Series: J-B Drucker Foundation Series, ISBN-13:9780787960704

Dweck, C. (2006). *Mindset: The new psychology of success.* New York: Random House.

Gladwell M, (2000). *The tipping Point,* Publisher: Little Brown ISBN 0-316-31696-2

Goleman, D, (1998) *Working with emotional intelligence.* New York: Bantam Books

Goleman D, Boyatzis R, McKee A, (2004) *Primal Leadership* HBS Press

Goleman D, (2001) *Leadership that gets results*, Harvard Business Review,

Hargreaves D, (2012) A self- improving school system: towards maturity. Published by DFE.

Hattie, J, (2008). *Visible Learning: A Synthesis of Over 800 Meta-Analyses Relating to Achievement.* NY: Routledge. ISBN 978-0-415-47618-8.

Herzberg, F, (1959). *The Motivation to Work.* New York: John Wiley and Sons, ISBN 978-1560006343

Joyce B, Showers B, (1988). *Student Achievement Through Staff Development: Fundamentals of School Renewal.* Longman.

Joyce B and Showers B, (1996). *The Evolution of Peer Coaching.* Educational Leadership.

Kotter J, (1996). *Leading Change.* Harvard Business School Press. ISBN 0875847471

Lewin K, (1951). *Field Theory in Social Science: Selected Theoretical Papers.* Harper & Row

Luft J, Ingham H, (1950) *The Johari Window - A graphic model of interpersonal awareness.* Proceedings of the Western Training laboratories in group development. UCLA

MacBeath J, (1999.) *School Must Speak for Themselves.* – Routledge ISBN 0-414-20580-8

Goldsmith M, internet article on Feedforward. http://www.culturechangega.org/special_projects/Feedforward%20by%20Marshall%20Goldsmith.pdf

Maslow A (1943). *A Theory of Human Motivation.* Psychological Review

Roberts K (1990). *Some characteristics of Highly reliable organisations.* Organisational Science

Rogers, E. (1962.) *Diffusion of Innovations.* Glencoe: Free Press.

Scholes K, Johnson G, Whittington R, (2002). *Exploring Corporate Strategy* Published by Financial Times. ISBN 970-0273711919

Scott S, (2002). *Fierce Conversations.* Publisher Judy Piatkuss ISBN 0670031240

Senge P, (1990). *The fifth discipline*, Doubleday/Currency. ISBN 0385260946

Southworth G, (2005). *The essentials of school leadership.* Sage Publications Ltd

Whitmore Sir J, (1984.) *Coaching for Performance.* Publisher Nicholas Brealey ISBN 1857883039

Printed in Great Britain
by Amazon